SPORT PSYCHOLOGY LIBRARY:

TRIATHLON

Praise for Sport Psychology Library: Triathlon

"Finally, a comprehensive sports psychology book that converts theory into practical and manageable exercises. Athletes can implement them and see immediate results as they work on the details that translate into success."

–Jamie Cleveland,
Ironman and Canadian National champion

"This is a great guide that will prove to be an invaluable resource to any triathlete looking to improve. This book is going to be a 'must-read' for all of the people I coach!"

–Kevin Mackinnon,
Canadian triathlon coach

"Finally a sports psychology book that takes into account the unique aspects and challenges that the sport of triathlon throws at the athlete. Looking back on my best races, they were always preceded by a strict regimen of mental training and preparation. However, when reading sports psychology books I was always reading about other sporting disciplines and trying to apply it to triathlon. It is nice to know that there is now a book dedicated to our sport. This book will now be in my arsenal of training equipment."

–Mike Neill,
elite professional Ironman triathlete

SPORT PSYCHOLOGY LIBRARY:

TRIATHLON

Joe Baker
YORK UNIVERSITY

Whitney Sedgwick
UNIVERSITY OF BRITISH COLUMBIA

Fitness Information Technology

A Division of the International Center for Performance Excellence
262 Coliseum, WVU-PE
P.O. Box 6116
Morgantown, WV 26506-6116

The sport psychological techniques or physical activities discussed in this book are not intended as a substitute for consultation with a sport psychologist or physician. Further, because people respond differently, it cannot be guaranteed that these psychological techniques will result in an improvement in sport performance. Readers are encouraged to contact the Association for the Advancement of Applied Sport Psychology, the American Psychological Association, or the United States Olympic Committee for further information about the delivery of sport psychology services.

Library of Congress Card Catalog Number: 2005921691

ISBN: 1885693621

Production Editor: Matt Brann
Cover Design: 40 West Studios
Typesetter: 40 West Studios
Copyeditor: Corey Madsen
Proofreader: Geoff Fuller
Indexer: Geoff Fuller
Printer: Data Reproductions

Cover photos © 2005, SportsChrome, Inc. All rights reserved.

10 9 8 7 6 5 4 3 2 1

Fitness Information Technology
A Division of the International Center for Performance Excellence
West Virginia University
262 Coliseum, WVU-PE
PO Box 6116
Morgantown, WV 26506-6116
800.477.4348 (toll free)
304.293.6888 (phone)
304.293.6658 (fax)
Email: icpe@mail.wvu.edu
Website: www.fitinfotech.com

It takes courage to push yourself to places that you have never been before ... to test your limits ... to break through barriers. And the day came when the risk it took to remain tight in the bud was more painful than the risk it took to blossom.

Anais Nin

Table of Contents

Preface

This book is designed for the progressive triathlete. Our purpose in writing is to fill a gap in current literature by focusing on the psychological components of successful triathlon performance. To date, the majority of practical information available to triathletes comes in the form of training manuals describing current (as well as out-of-date) training practices that focus on the physical aspects of triathlon training. This is in light of the admission by many top triathletes that success is often determined by mental or psychological attributes rather than physical ones.

In order to achieve our purpose, an integrated approach is presented where current research assists the development of practical exercises to enhance triathlon-relevant psychological capacities. Psychological aspects of triathlon performance are considered in detail; specifically, chapters examine the basic sport psychology concepts of goal setting, arousal management, focus/concentration during competition, as well as imagery and visualization. Dealing with injuries that occur through training and competition and the role of reflection are especially relevant to triathlon competition. These areas are given particular attention in chapters 6 and 7. Our final chapter provides guidelines for starting and adhering to a psychological skills program.

Each chapter uses current research in the topic area as the basis for the exercises, which are designed to facilitate the development of skills in a specific area of psychological development. Utilizing current research from sport psychology labs around the world allows us to present useful and practical information that is rooted in current psychological theory.

This book contains several unique features. First, to our knowledge it is the only book to solely examine the psychological components of triathlon training and competition. Second, the topics chosen for inclusion were generated through focus group discussions with current triathletes of all ability levels. This allowed us to identify and present relevant issues that may be useful to a significant majority of athletes rather than specific concerns relevant to a few elite athletes. Lastly, the integration of current research and practical exercises provides a foundation for creating athletes that are informed and capable of using aspects of sport psychology to manage their performance in triathlon and other domains; it may be this last characteristic that is the most salient.

Acknowledgments

Like most books, the names on the front cover do not denote all those who have contributed to its creation. First and foremost, we need to acknowledge the hard work and creativity of the sport psychologists who were our teachers. The majority of the information contained in this book has been the direct result of seeds planted by others. Some of the exercises in this book are modified or adapted versions developed by others, and while the community of sport psychology is wonderful for sharing ideas, it makes it difficult to track an idea to its origin. We have tried to acknowledge appropriate sources in our further readings section, but in the event that errors exist, we accept full blame and extend our deepest apologies. We would also like to thank those who were kind enough to read preliminary versions of the chapters in this book and to provide honest and constructive feedback. Many also provided the pictures contained within. These individuals include Ann-Marie Kungl, Jennifer Robertson-Wilson, Rob Wilson, Michelle Smith, Jessica Fraser-Thomas, Andrew Fishpool, Andy Wright, Steve Cobley, Valerie Hadd, and Cathi Sabiston. As well, the professional reviewers provided thoughtful comments that resulted in a more comprehensive book. We would also like to thank our illustrator, Alexandra Weir, for her excellent work. We extend our heartfelt gratitude to our families for the love and support they have provided in this and other undertakings. Finally, we give credit and thanks to each other—years of genuine professional collegiality, rich discussions, and friendship made writing this book a pleasure.

Joe Baker, PhD
Whitney Sedgwick, PhD, R.Psych.

1

THE START LINE: INTRODUCTION AND OVERVIEW OF THE PSYCHOLOGY OF THE TRIATHLON

I think you can talk yourself into, or out of, almost anything. Triathletes are especially good at both, and they can swing from one extreme to another several times during a race. There are physical fears to conquer, like heavy surf and cold ocean water or a fast downhill turn on the bike (or dusty roads), and mental mountains of endurance to climb as well. The winners, sometimes just the finishers, are those who are able to maintain the necessary level of confidence, composure, and concentration from start to finish. There is no place for self-doubt in a triathlon, yet self-doubt runs rampant through the ranks of even the best. It's a problem that strong arms and legs are only partially capable of solving.

Scott Tinley

Consider whether any of the following circumstances apply to you:

- You trained all year for a particular race only to feel dissatisfied with your result because you know you could have done better.

- You never seem to perform as well in competition as you do in training.

- You find it difficult to maintain focus at key points during the race.

- You lack motivation to train without your training partner(s).

- You have several nagging injuries that interfere with training and competition.

If you have experienced any of the scenarios listed above, then this book can provide the elusive answers to your questions. In all sports there's a delicate balance between training that is optimal for the physical and psychological modifications necessary for performance improvements and training too much. If an optimal balance is not maintained, due to either physical or cognitive reasons, performance suffers. This is especially true in sports like the triathlon, where performance improvement is achieved by subjecting the body and mind to extreme amounts of stress.

It's human nature to challenge the limits of our physical and mental abilities. It is this drive that led to the creation of the triathlon in the early 1970s. Since its inception, the sport of triathlon has gained tremendous momentum, evolving from a sport largely performed by a small number of "super-humans" to its current status as a mainstream, mass-participation sport. Perhaps the crowning achievement of triathlons' evolution has been its inclusion in the 2000 Olympic Games in Sydney, Australia.

Although the sport of triathlon is still in its infancy, it has a rich history of heroes. People like Dave Scott, Mark Allen, Scott Tinley, Scott Molina, Mike Pigg, Paula Newby-Fraser, and Erin Baker conjure up memories of triathlon's golden days of the 1980s and early '90s, while names like Peter Reid, Tim DeBoom, Simon Whitfield, Natasha Badmann, Michellie Jones, and Lori Bowden remind us that the legacy of triathlon is only just beginning. Clearly, it is an exciting time to be a triathlete, whether you are an international competitor, a first-time sprint triathlete, or at any level in between.

Training for triathlons leads to somewhat of a paradox: triathletes usually enjoy the challenge of strenuous competition but want to make the event as effortless as possible through appropriate training beforehand. The elements that go into achieving triathlon success are as varied as the participants themselves. However, some common characteristics exist. Superior physical fitness is an obvious necessity, but high levels of muscular and cardiovascular strength and endurance do not fully account for successful performance in the triathlon. Few would argue that successful triathlon performance is also the result of superior mental fitness, including the ability to maintain proper focus, manage physical pain, set appropriate goals, and maintain high levels of motivation. Oddly, this aspect of triathlon performance is rarely addressed.

Figure 1 presents an integrated model of triathlon performance incorporating elements thought to be influential in predicting performance. These elements can be grouped under two broad headings: physical and cognitive. As a triathlete, physical variables are probably very familiar to you. Exercise physiologists have indicated that physical elements such as aerobic capacity (VO_2max), movement efficiency, and body composition are good predictors of endurance performance. Cognitive elements may be a bit less familiar to some readers. Cognition refers to the process of knowing, which can involve reasoning and judgment. Thoughts fall in the cognitive realm as well.

Less is known about the role that cognitive variables play in successful performance; however, research from the discipline of sport psychology indicates that cognitive fitness is also influential in determining performance. Moreover, it is now known that these two groups of variables (the physical and cognitive) are not distinct and that both interact to create successful performers. Studies have shown that belief in your ability to accomplish a task can have a positive effect on performance. For example, in a study of British weight lifters, athletes who were given a placebo but told they were taking steroid supplements achieved significant performance gains. At the mid-point of the study, half of the participants were informed that they had taken a placebo and performance in this group returned to normal levels. This research is just one example that solidly supports the link between athletes' beliefs during both training and competition and their ultimate performance. Studies on the effects of self-talk (see Chapter 4 for more on this topic) provide similar evidence of the interrelationship between cognitive processes and physical performance. Simply put, the power of positive thinking should not be underestimated.

Numerous texts are available that examine the physical aspects of triathlon performance, and a brief list is presented in the *Further Reading* section of this book. These books and research articles generally provide a competent description of the physical aspects of triathlon training and competition. However, the primary focus of this book is on the cognitive component of the model presented in Figure 1. Let's now turn to what we do know about the psychological elements of high-level athletes, including triathletes.

Psychological Characteristics of Elite Athletes

Research into the psychological attributes of champion athletes has suggested that elite athletes share a number of psychological dispositions. In general, elite athletes possess greater self-confidence, have less anxiety during and prior to competition, have greater concentration on goals and movements, have a better ability to cope with poor performance, and think in much more positive ways.

Triathletes are exceptionally good at training their bodies to accommodate the physical aspects of triathlon performance. On the other hand, few athletes consider training for the cognitive aspects of performance. One of the underlying principles on which this book is based is that *mental skills, like physical skills, are learned and perfected through purposeful training.*

Figure 1.1: Physical and Cognitive Variables Affecting Triathlon Performance

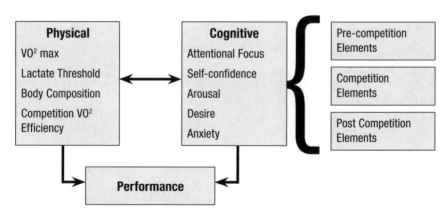

It is a common misconception that successful athletes are born with the abilities that make them successful. Successful endurance athletes are often referred to as having a 'killer instinct' that allows them to succeed under competitive situations. The ability to focus under pressure or deal with anxiety is commonly misconstrued as being an innate skill. Actually, recent research indicates that athletes in possession of these enviable capacities likely acquired them through dedicated practice rather than being born with them. Recent research from our lab examining the development of elite Ironman triathletes indicates that specific skills required for success in triathlon are highly sport-specific and can only be acquired through numerous hours of training. As succinctly stated by Vidal Sassoon, (yes, *that* Vidal Sassoon) "The only place success comes before work is in the dictionary."

What is Sport Psychology?

Collectively, the term *sport psychology* refers to all cognitive aspects of sport participation, ranging from broad concepts such as the psychological benefits of sport involvement (e.g., increased self-esteem) to specific items like the effects of pre-competition routines on forms of anxiety. Sport psychologists examine human behavior in sport and strive to help athletes and coaches apply relevant knowledge within sport settings. However, this book has a very applied focus and will examine a component of sport psychology referred to as psychological skills training (PST). PST is specifically related to the cognitive variables associated with human performance. For example, how does nervousness before a race influence your ability to get into your optimal performance zone? Or, does arriving early to the race better prepare you for the day's competition? These are just two of the questions that fall within the realm of PST.

It has been our experience that some athletes are resistant to sport psychology. Whether this is because they believe that answers to performance issues can only be resolved through increases or modifications to their physical training regimens or because they believe that sport psychology is a 'bunch of hocus pocus' is unknown. However, we would like to clarify two of the more common misconceptions about sport psychology and its value to triathletes.

Misconception #1–Sport psychology is touchy-feely rubbish that is useless in real sports.

In actuality, sport psychology principles and guidelines are grounded in applied and laboratory research, just like physiological principles. Today, research in sport psychology is scientifically reliable, and sport psychology has taken its place as a valid discipline in the field of kinesiology. Sport psychology has incorporated elements from the sport sciences (such as exercise physiology and biomechanics) and from psychology (such as the developmental and counseling subdomains). Many of the exercises and issues identified in this book were generated through focus groups with current triathletes from various levels. We have attempted to provide information that is relevant and the result of current psychological theory.

Misconception #2–Sport psychology is only useful for elite athletes.

This misconception is simply not true. Athletes of all levels have used sport psychology principles to achieve performance improvements. It is helpful if you think of forms of mental training as similar to forms of physical training. Just as running intervals can help athletes of all ages and ability levels, learning to maintain focus or manage arousal during competition can also improve performance in triathletes of all ages and ability levels.

You may notice that although the exercises we provide are specific to triathlon training and competition, they can easily be adapted to fit other areas of your life. Anxiety, imagery, and arousal are psychological factors

Tell me about your relationship with your mother

encountered under performance conditions regardless of whether you are racing or speaking at a board meeting. We encourage you to take the exercises described in this book and apply them to your daily living outside of triathlon.

How to Use This Book

It is our assumption in writing this book that those who are reading it are willing to try the exercises provided in each chapter. Ideally, this book will allow you to become more familiar with the principles of sport psychology, particularly as they apply to your triathlon training and performance. This book *should not* be seen as a substitute for a qualified sport psychologist. Acquiring a competent personal sport psychologist would likely be far more beneficial than any book could ever attempt to be. As we have already mentioned and will continue to mention throughout this book, each individual athlete is highly complex. Consequently, the skills necessary for successful performance for one athlete are not necessarily the skills required by another. We are aware that the majority of triathletes are not able or inclined to use the services of a personal sport psychologist. Therefore, we have attempted to provide exercises that are applicable to triathletes of all ages and ability levels. You can copy the pages to use again if you want to measure your progress over time, or to make handouts for others. This way you can try the techniques and adapt them to accommodate your specific needs.

With the exception of the introduction and concluding chapters, each chapter is centered on a specific topic of triathlon psychology. Exercises are presented to help you develop specific psychological skills to be used in the appropriate situations. Collectively, the book presents a detailed plan for developing and integrating psychological skills. We encourage you to sample and modify the skills to create a plan that is tailored to your needs. Ready? Let's get started.

CHAPTER SUMMARY

• Athletes of any ability level can use sport psychology to maximize performance.

• Mental skills need to be learned and perfected through purposeful training over extended periods of time.

PRE-COMPETITION AND TRAINING FACTORS

SECTION I

While the most obvious effects of solid mental preparation are manifested in successful competition, the real work is done in training. This section examines techniques to utilize the time you have in the preseason to maximize performance during the competitive season. The first chapter in this section discusses how to increase your motivation through proper goal setting. The second chapter examines the value of imagery in augmenting performance.

2

"I WANT TO GO FAST ..." MOTIVATION AND GOAL SETTING FOR MAXIMIZED INVOLVEMENT

I've always believed that if you put in the work, the results will come. I don't do things halfheartedly, because I know if I do, then I can expect halfhearted results. That's why I approached practices the same way I approached games. You can't turn it on and off like a faucet. I couldn't dog it during practice and then, when I need that extra push late in the game, expect it to be there.

Michael Jordan

Have you ever considered why you do the things you do? Although this could be construed as a rather deep question, think about it for a moment. Why do you get up when it is still dark, and willingly put yourself through hours of intense physical effort? How do you get yourself to step into that frigid lake to log more (cold) open-water miles? Answers to these questions provide important information about what motivates you.

Stripped of all the jargon, the basis for *motivation theory* is that we are driven to perform activities that we feel are meeting our needs, and we disengage from activities that don't meet these needs. The term *motivation* refers to a state of activation or interest that helps direct and sustain behavior. The factors that can affect your level of motivation are typically broken down into one of two categories. The first is internal elements, such as partaking in an activity for the sheer enjoyment of the task, feelings of pride, and accomplishment (categorized as *intrinsic* factors). The second category is made up of elements that are outside of us, such as receiving rewards, trophies, T-shirts, money, and other people's approval (categorized as *extrinsic* factors). Consider the following categories as well:

Social reasons (*to spend time with friends, to be part of a group*)

Competitive reasons (*to win trophies and medals*)

Proficiency reasons (*to become more skilled, to get faster*)

Emotional reasons (*to have fun, enjoyment*)

Health reasons (*to get fitter, healthier*)

Think for a moment of the factors that motivate you to train and compete in triathlons. You can use the following form to record these factors, both intrinsic and extrinsic.

Training

Intrinsic motivators	Extrinsic motivators
_____	_____
_____	_____
_____	_____

Competition

Intrinsic motivators	Extrinsic motivators
_____	_____
_____	_____
_____	_____

Which of the four lists contains the most points? What does this say to you regarding your personal motivation to train and race? Keep these factors in mind as we progress through this chapter. They provide essential information about your motivational profile.

Attributions

A critical aspect of motivation theory that has important implications for athletes concerns how you explain your success and failure. To what factors are you *attributing* your performance? These factors generally concern three areas (Figure 2.1). *Stability* refers to whether you are attributing your success or failure to factors that are relatively unchanging (such as your ability) or factors that are unpredictable (such as luck). The *locus of causality* refers to whether you are attributing the cause of your success or failure to an internal or external factor. For example, after a successful performance in your local triathlon, you could attribute your success to your optimal preparation for this race (an internal cause) or the relatively easy field of competitors (an external cause). Finally, *locus of control* refers to whether the factors are in or out of your control. For example, you have significant control over your training but very little control over the weather, yet each can have a significant effect on performance.

Figure 2.1: Attribution Categories

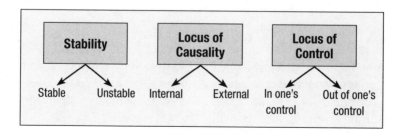

Research generally indicates that attributing performance to certain types of stable factors leads to increased expectations for future success. Note that stable factors mean they are unlikely to change over time. Consider a study conducted in Australia a few years ago, which asked Australian athletes and coaches to identify the factors responsible for the dominance of Australians in swimming and East Africans in middle distance running. The athletes and coaches reported that Australian dominance in swimming was attributed to unstable factors such as training and preparation, while East African dominance was attributed to stable factors such as superior genetic ability (e.g., the belief that East Africans are genetically superior runners). How do you think these attributions affect athletes' expectations for success or desire to train? Can you name some stable and unstable factors that could contribute to your triathlon performance?

Now let's consider your attributions. Think back to a recent competition where you had a successful race. Make a list of reasons that contributed to your success. Explain why you were successful in this race. Now think back to a race where you were unsuccessful and make a list of reasons explaining this lack of success. Compare your list of attributes. Are they stable or unstable, internal or external, in your control or out of your control? Have these attributions affected your approach to training or competition in any way? Attributing your success to stable, internal factors that are within your control can lead to increased expectations for success in the future. They can also lead to increased feelings of pride and accomplishment as well as increased motivation. On the other hand, attributing your failures to stable, internal factors that are within your control can have the opposite effect (expectations of failure, feelings of shame, and decreased motivation). Be aware of the factors that you think are contributing to your successful and unsuccessful performances. They could have significant influence on your desire for, and intensity during, training and competition.

Goal Orientation

Another factor that can affect your motivation is whether you have adopted a *competitive* or a *mastery* goal orientation. Competition goals (also referred to as outcome goals) involve focusing on defeating others or winning trophies/awards, while mastery goals (also referred to as task goals) involve focusing on improving relative to your previous performance. Motivation researchers agree there are benefits to maintaining a mastery orientation over a competitive orientation. Mastery orientations have been found to lead to more persistence and better performance. Mastery orientations also provide greater control, which has a positive influence on motivation. Competitive orientations, on the other hand, can lead to disappointment, frustration, and decreased motivation when the performance of others is superior to

*If one advances confidently in the direction of his
dreams, and endeavors to live the life he has imagined,
he will meet with success unexpected in common hours.*

Henry David Thoreau

yours. Always judging success relative to the performance of others is also potentially damaging to your sense of self-worth.

Goal Setting

An area of sport psychology that is very closely linked to motivation is goal setting. The importance of establishing clear goals can positively affect motivation. Perhaps one of the most compelling examples of the value of goal setting is Olympic swimmer John Naber. Naber calculated that he needed to drop four seconds off his best time to break the world record in the backstroke in four years. In order to achieve this goal he determined that he needed to "drop one second per year, or one-tenth of a second per month, or $1/300^{th}$ of a second per day, or $1/1200^{th}$ of a second for each hour of training." By breaking a somewhat daunting long-term goal into manageable chunks, Naber was able to work at achieving his objective. This is just one way to establish achievable goals using time. Likely, across varied situations, too many factors may make over-reliance on time goals unrealistic (i.e., weather, injury, course conditions). Instead of setting a goal based on the clock, you can establish personal goals related to specific training elements. A goal of maintaining proper form during a particularly difficult portion of the run could be an example.

Setting goals involves clarifying expectations and mapping out plans to success. In this chapter we discuss the benefits of goal setting and provide guidelines for establishing training, competition, and personal goals. Goal setting can enhance performance, facilitate more effective training sessions, and increase personal feelings of pride, motivation, satisfaction, and self-confidence. When done correctly, goal setting can also increase your level of enjoyment during a task, even potentially mundane tasks like tuning your bike or long, slow distance swims in the pool.

Goal setting can simply be described as attaining a specific standard of proficiency, usually within a standard time limit, and should be viewed as a dynamic, never-ending process. Establishing and working toward goals is common practice in professional organizations, in educational settings, even in personal relationships. The common element across these different settings is that our mental (and physical) resources are directed toward a desired end result.

Damon Burton, a sport psychologist at the University of Idaho, has referred to the "Jekyll and Hyde nature" of goal setting. This means that it is important to set goals properly, otherwise the goals can actually inhibit motivation and performance. There are several potential hazards related to poorly set goals, which can spell disaster for the athlete. Later in this chapter we'll focus on how to set goals that maximize intrinsic (internal) motivation and optimize the likelihood of successful performance. Goals that are properly set are more likely to mobilize your efforts, increase your persistence, and motivate the search for appropriate task strategies. For example, if you know you are recovering from an injury, but plan to compete in a half-Ironman in one month, your goals should accurately reflect your physical and psychological stages of recovery.

Goal setting works by focusing and directing activity and regulating effort expenditure. Establishing goals also enhances persistence and promotes the development of new strategies for improving performance.

Interestingly, there are a multitude of types of goals. There are long-, short-, and intermediate-term goals, which are defined by the time frame in which you hope to achieve them. These time frames are fairly self-explanatory, with room for individual interpretation. For some athletes, the short term would be by the end of tomorrow, while for others it could be next Friday. Long-term goals could be one year from today or five years from today. You may set a long-term training goal for one year from today, for example, of competing in your first half-Ironman race. These goals can then be set in a variety of ways:

- *Process goals* focus on your ongoing performance, and can be physical, psychological, technical, and/or strategic in nature (e.g., focusing on the specifics of your running form during a run)

- *Outcome goals* are geared toward the anticipated or desired end result (e.g., goal to finish in the top 25 competitors of a certain race)

- *Seasonal goals* are devised around the training calendar year (e.g., "I would like to race three times this summer")

- *Lifestyle goals* concern your health habits (e.g., diet, sleeping patterns, social supports)

Using the form below, write out two goals for each section (an example is provided in the first line of each section), then consider what category of goal this would be and record beside the goal. When you are done, take a look at your responses and note which goals come easiest to you. Are you more focused on the long-term results? Are you a results-oriented person (outcome goals)? Or are you more focused on your entire life and balancing physical activity with family, etc? Is there a pattern to your goals? If so, would it be to your advantage to develop and implement progress toward goals in the other areas?

In sport you can also establish *training* and *competition* goals. When you consider the variety of goal types, it becomes clear just how many facets of training and competition can be affected by goal setting.

Short-term goals

(i.e., to be completed by 5 p.m. tomorrow)

- To finish 10 km time-trial in under 44:30 (outcome)
- _____
- _____

Intermediate-term goals

(i.e., to be completed by one month from today—and write date)

- To have consulted with sport nutritionist once and begun seeing chiropractor once a week (lifestyle)
- _____
- _____

Long-term goals

(i.e., to be completed one year from today—and write date)

- Devised and recorded complete monthly swim training program on wall calendar (seasonal and process)
- _____
- _____

Whether you think you can or think you can't, you're probably right ...

Anonymous

There are some important points to consider for general goal setting. First, it is best to tailor your goals specifically to your aspirations. This means you may not be able to simply adopt your training partner's goals (at least not all of them) and be totally effective. For example, when running intervals with your running group, set your split times (your goal) relative to your own abilities and not someone else's. While we may share some similarities with our training partners, it is important to acknowledge and work with our unique differences as well.

Second, goals should be specific. Specific goals direct activity more  effectively and reliably than vague goals. Research indicates that they lead to better performance than nebulous goals, such as to "do your best." It's also important to set practice goals within simulated performance conditions. As an example, let's consider a goal that you might have for the swim portion of an upcoming race. How many minutes (and seconds) do you plan for the swim leg? How would your goal change if it were raining on race day? What is a realistic time in these weather conditions? Quantifying goals (under a variety of possible conditions) makes them more effective, so putting a time estimate on each component of the race is important to remember when establishing effective performance goals.

Lastly, goals must be adequately challenging. Difficult or challenging goals produce better performances than moderate or easy goals, assuming you possess sufficient ability and commitment. Research indicates that setting goals that have a 50% probability of success is more effective than goals that are either too easy or too difficult. For example, if you currently run 10 kilometers in 55 minutes, setting a goal of 50 minutes will lead to greater persistence than a goal of 35 minutes.

Your commitment to a task is also affected by your level of goal acceptance, participation in setting the goal (e.g., with the coach), and your incentive toward the goal. Also, giving yourself rewards can positively influence your commitment to training. When you do these things to increase your commitment, you are engaging in goal setting. An added bonus is that effective goals can, in turn, positively affect your self-confidence. Athletes with high self-confidence are more likely to persist toward their goals over longer periods of time.

However, optimal goal setting also requires timely *feedback* showing progression toward the goal. Every time you glance at your watch on a run, you get feedback about your performance and how close you are to a time and/or distance goal for that day. Competition is a form of feedback that informs you about your current level of development and can lead to the setting of higher goals and increases in goal commitment.

Feedback can come in verbal, nonverbal, and/or written forms. If your coach gives you positive encouragement (e.g., "Excellent, that's the way!"), that's verbal feedback. Nonverbal feedback is most commonly seen in body language or facial expressions; so, if your training partner has arms crossed and won't look at you, perhaps he or she is bothered by something! Lastly, written questionnaires or evaluation forms can also provide useful feedback. You and your coach might each decide to complete written summaries of your training progress—these would be examples of written feedback. Typically, you and your coach would determine at the beginning of a training season the frequency and timing of evaluations. For example, you may agree on skill(s) to focus on preseason, and then complete the form at the middle and end of the preseason to monitor progress. An example of this type of form can be found on the following page.

This form can be completed in point form or in sentences, depending on the athlete's style (a combination approach was used in the example).

The same form could be completed by the coach and compared with the athlete's version.

There are some common errors to avoid when establishing goals. The first is setting too many goals too soon. In training, begin with one or two clear goals in mind. A second error is setting goals that are too general or vague, such as the vague title of this chapter. It is better to be specific when determining your goals. Also, if you set a goal and do not attain it, you may need to modify the goal. It may be unrealistic for you at this stage of your training or level of experience. Failing to create a supportive environment in which to strive toward your goals is another common mistake. For example, if you have a training goal of improving the arm mechanics of your front crawl, hiring a coach to work with you on technique would be a more supportive solution than training alone.

Specific goal: *(e.g., to improve 40 km time trial time)*
Date: (write today's date)
Training period dates (from - to): *01/01/05-04/01/05*

PRESEASON

What needs to be done to advance toward this goal:

1. *weight training sessions 3x per week to build muscle strength and power*
2. *riding indoors at least 3x per week to keep aerobic conditioning*
3. *continue seeing physiotherapist bi-monthly to monitor chronic quad injury*

Progress toward preseason goals (completed at middle of the preseason):

1. *Good. I kept up with the 3x per week weights sessions with the exception of one week in February due to vacation. Progress is going well. I increased weights and reps on all activities.*
2. *I kept riding indoors all winter with only a couple of misses (3x because of work and other commitments).*
3. *I have attended all physiotherapist appointments, less pain in quads.*

END OF PRESEASON: *(fill out this section at end of 04/05)*

Overall Evaluation:
Overall, feel good about progress. I am anxious to get on the roads. My legs have gotten much stronger over the winter, and I feel fitter than ever. Plus, the sessions at the physiotherapist have my leg feeling better than it has in years.

A last error is when people set inaccurate goals that are inappropriate for them. Being honest with yourself about your capabilities will aid in more accurate personal goals.

A goal is only worthy of the effort to achieve it.

Kate Pace, Canadian
Olympic skier

In their book *The Mental Game Plan*, sport psychologists Stephen Bull, John Albinson, and Chris Shambrook suggest one simple way to ensure that you are setting effective goals is to implement the SMART program. Other researchers, Edwin Locke, Gary Latham, and colleagues, have extended this to SMARTER (see exercise later in this chapter). This straightforward acronym contains all of the useful information we have discussed so far with respect to goal setting.

Writing down your goals will help hold you accountable. Some people like to post goals where they know they will see them, such as in their equipment bag or gym locker. Reading your own words can bolster your mind and spirit before training and competition. Here is a quick exercise you can try right now. Take out a sheet of paper and write down two short-term and two long-term triathlon goals. For the purposes of this exercise, let's say that short-term is for one month from today and long-term is six months from today. Now using the following acronym of SMARTER goals, review your goals and make appropriate adjustments.

Devise short-term goals that can be used as a means to obtain long-term goals. A goal to improve your run time by 10 seconds/week in order to shave 40 seconds off your time over the next month would be an example. A goal to read this sport psychology triathlon book by the end of the week and to have incorporated four exercises into your training regime by the end of next month is also an example. This is better than using long-term goals alone, as it allows you to keep track of your progress. In essence, you have a plan or strategy.

Now that you are familiar with some of the background theory on goal setting and motivation, begin by establishing where you are at the present moment. Are there certain areas that you would like to improve? What about areas of your training where you are satisfied with your current performance? How can you continue to stay at that level or look

Specific
>Is your goal clear and concise?

Measurable
>Can you determine whether you've achieved the goal? (yes/no)

Attainable
>Have you considered factors out of your control and made allowances for them (e.g., catching the flu could affect your training progress)?

Realistic
>Is the goal appropriate for level of fitness, accessibility of resources, etc.?

Time-phased
>Is progress and ultimate attainment of the goal measurable in minutes, hours, days, or months?

Exciting
>Are you both enjoying the process and looking forward to achieving your established product goal?

Recorded
>Have you written down your goal?

to make further improvements? This strategy requires you to set aside some quiet time to think about these questions. Writing down your ideas and responses can allow ongoing review as your training and abilities progress to higher levels. Many athletes keep journals and/or training logs; these books are great for recording physical, technical, *and* psychological observations. Trying out the exercises in this chapter and then revisiting them over time will help to inform your current and future training.

Use your training log to keep track of your goals. They can be subdivided into technical, physical, and mental goals. Also, break general goals (for example, to become a more technically proficient swimmer) into specifics so that you can brainstorm strategies to move toward goal attainment (e.g., get stroke tips from local coach, swim 3x/week for 45 minutes, alternating the focus of the workouts). Also, don't forget

Into your hands will be placed the exact result of your thoughts, you will receive that which you earn, no more, no less.

Source unknown

target dates (e.g., will call new running coach by this Saturday). Use your training log as a means of recording and implementing your goal-setting program.

It may be helpful to adopt the strategies of a news reporter. Just like sleuthing for a good story, you can provide yourself with the answers to the "5 Ws and the H." The Who is easy (you) but the others require a bit more work—What (are you trying to accomplish?), Where (will movement toward this goal take place?), Why (are you working toward this particular goal?), When (are you planning to have this goal accomplished?), and How (are you going to plan for this goal?). These are each applicable and valid questions that should be considered when establishing short-, intermediate-, and long-term goals.

State your goals from a positive perspective. So, instead of saying, "I will not go too slow and be a wimp on the bike turns," you can say to yourself, "When it comes to the bike turns, I will be smooth and consistently in control." If you use negative language, such as "I will not make a mistake," you are actually more likely to make a mistake. It is far more empowering when you speak in positive, encouraging terms. This can be linked back to focusing on the positive when recording your progress in your journal or training log.

In summary, setting goals depends to a large extent on your level of motivation. You've read of the many different types of goals and perhaps have already begun to prioritize which are important to you at this stage. There are many theories exploring how individuals set goals and what motivates people toward achievement and performance—we've only covered a few in this chapter. More important are the strategies that can help you to achieve your many goals, be they short-, intermediate-, long-term, process, product and/ or outcome goals. The above strategies can be implemented at your discretion. Also note the need for feedback. Remember, whether it's verbal, nonverbal (i.e., body language), and/or written feedback, it is an important resource toward monitoring whether or not you are on the right track toward your goals.

CHAPTER HIGHLIGHTS

- Be aware of the specific intrinsic or extrinsic factors that drive your training and competition.

- Consider the attributes you use to explain your successful or unsuccessful performances.

- Attributing success to stable, internal factors within your control can lead to increased expectations of success in the future.

- Mastery goals have a more positive effect on our motivation than competitive goals.

- Short- and long-term goals should be used to plan and evaluate progress.

- Goals should be SMARTER (specific, measurable, attainable, realistic, time-based, exciting, and recorded).

- Use your training log to keep track of your goals.

- Be positive when thinking and recording your goals.

3

USING ALL OF YOUR SENSES: IMAGERY

I never hit a shot, even in practice, without having a very sharp, in-focus picture of it in my head. It's like a color movie... just make sure your movies show a perfect shot. We don't want any horror films of shots flying into sand or water or out of bounds.

Jack Nicklaus

Most people don't realize that they use imagery almost daily. For example, you probably used imagery this morning to pick out the clothes you are now wearing. When it comes to triathlon training, the likelihood that you've used imagery in the past (without even knowing it) is quite high. For example, "seeing yourself" climbing a steep hill represents naturally occurring, covert imagery. However, this differs from the systematic, logical use of this skill. The latter depends in part on the abilities and goals of the individual athlete and is the focus of this chapter.

Imagery is considered one of the most basic mental training skills; the concept is discussed in virtually every sport psychology text. As a training tool, athletes use imagery for general performance enhancement and for more specific purposes. Sport psychologists Terry Orlick and John Partington reported that 99% of athletes surveyed at the 1984 Los Angeles Olympic Games used imagery 4x/week (average of 12 minutes per session) in a systematic, pre-planned manner. More

recently, 90% of athletes at the United States Olympic Center report using imagery in training and competition. In this chapter, you'll learn how to apply the mental skill of imagery to various aspects of triathlon performance and acquire many tips to hone your personal imagery ability level.

Before going any further, let's define the term. Imagery has been described as both an art and a science, and is often used interchangeably with terms like mental rehearsal, mental practice, and visualization. Some argue that visualization is an incomplete term that implies that you are only seeing yourself performing the skill/activity. Since we have five senses, imagery may be better defined as using all of your senses to create or recreate an experience in your mind. Another way to put it is that imagery is training your muscles to know they've been in the situation before. Imagery has also been described as a symbolic sensory experience.

Imagery is not the same as your mind wandering or daydreaming. When employing imagery, you are consciously aware of the experience, which makes imagery different than idle daydreaming. Another consideration is that you do not need any external stimuli to use the mental skill. For example, you don't need a bicycle to implement imagery training in order to improve your cycling ability—imagery can be practiced virtually anywhere. Imagery can also complement your physical training in multiple ways. Research has shown that mental practice is better than no practice at all and that mental practice combined and alternated with physical practice is better than either alone. This means, for example, that if you are injured, utilizing imagery could be very beneficial to your recovery and a key part of the rehabilitation process (more on this in Chapter 6).

There are many ways for imagery to enhance your triathlon performance. By seeing yourself succeeding and reaching personal goals, and by physically feeling yourself doing so, you gain self-confidence. If you have been injured or have been experiencing a training slump, employing imagery can also help overcome these negative phases. Imagery is also an excellent tool for focusing attention, whether it is on your coach's instructions or navigating a bottleneck at the bike turnaround.

One of the early theoretical explanations of imagery focused on neuromuscular activation. Neuromuscular theories are based on the notion that "imaging" yourself performing an action activates the same neuromuscular pathways as actually performing the skill. Although the level of neuromuscular activation is low, it is still stimulating the same pathways used during performance. Some of the most convincing research supporting this theory comes from work done by Richard Suinn. In one study, he measured muscle movements in an injured skier's quadriceps muscle while the skier "imaged" a ski run. Results showed the muscles were firing in the same pattern as if the skier were actually skiing that particular run. The key difference was that his legs were not moving! Moving away from theory, what is clear is that imagery is a skill that many athletes use to promote optimal performance.

There are two main forms of imagery: internal and external. An internal imagery perspective involves using imagery as if you are actually in the situation. So, imaging standing on the pool deck and feeling the prickly floor beneath your toes, the tightness of your swim cap, the smell of the chlorine, and the color of the water is a complete example of internal imagery. The key here is that you are feeling these sensations from within your body. People have natural preferences toward one perspective over the other. Also, a triathlete might favor an external perspective while running, but use more of an internal vantage point when imaging the swimming leg of the race.

According to research, use of this kinesthetic viewpoint is more realistic in both training and competition. For example, Alison White and Lew Hardy, sport researchers in Wales, studied imagery use in sports that are influenced by environmental conditions. Their work suggests that for sports where perception (versus form) is important to successful execution, using internal imagery is more beneficial than an external viewpoint. Although the skills required for success in the triathlon are repetitive and not overly complex, outside elements still have the potential to influence

performance. Therefore, it's more useful to image yourself as if you were actually experiencing the sensations of performance.

Conversely, if you adopt an external perspective you are, to paraphrase golfer Jack Nicklaus, watching yourself in a movie. You are seeing yourself from an outside vantage point. At times this viewpoint can be helpful, particularly for refining technical awareness and proper skill. For example, you might have a coach videotape your swim stroke and then watch the tape together. This way, specific elements can be assessed. You can get useful feedback by analyzing these images of yourself, and this knowledge can then be filtered back into your kinesthetic or body awareness to improve future performance. This type of detailed analysis is optimal for skills that do not require much attention (i.e., they are well learned). If you are just learning how to swim, much of your attentional resources will be devoted to the mechanics of performing this motor skill, and you won't have time to attend to more minute details. So, the key is to learn the mechanics first and, once your technique is sound, you can incorporate imagery.

The optimal times to use imagery should also be considered. Imagery can be used both before and after performance. Imagery can help you envision how you want to perform, and to review how you actually did perform. In addition to using imagery at competitions, you may also find it beneficial to practice your skills at other times. Some athletes close their eyes while riding the bus to  work and do a brief imagery exercise. Frequently, athletes use the time before falling asleep at night, when they are physically and mentally relaxed. The importance of being relaxed and calm before attempting to use imagery cannot be understated. There will be more on relaxation later in this chapter.

When using imagery, it is important to fully optimize the experience. The elements of vividness, controllability, and emotionality/self-perception are essential. Vividness refers to incorporating all the details of the setting into your "image." For instance, try recalling the period right before the gun went off in your last race. What color socks were you wearing? Can you hear the sound of the people watching? Does your throat feel dry?

Being able to control the images you choose to experience is also crucial. Perhaps you want to improve your swimming stroke and have decided to use imagery as a mental training technique. Do you think it will ultimately help you in the pool if you use imagery and see yourself performing the stroke poorly? Not likely! In order to benefit, you want to mentally practice executing the proper technique. There are times when athletes use imagery first to see a technique the way they have currently been performing, then imaging correct execution of the skill, followed by repeating the motions in the correct fashion.

The last element, emotionality, is particularly important. Too often athletes don't incorporate feelings into their mental experience. You undoubtedly feel a variety of emotions throughout a given day, and these are hard to shut off when you set out for training. It's likely even harder to control the thoughts in anxiety-provoking situations like competitions. Recognizing the gamut of feelings as normal can help you to then use imagery to cope with naturally occurring emotions. So, knowing that you will likely experience some nerves before a race and incorporating the related physiological and emotional components into your imagery beforehand will better equip you when it comes to race day.

Integrating Imagery into Your Training/Competition

In order to fully experience and benefit from the use of imagery techniques, begin experiencing all of your senses as a simple exercise. Practice this on both training days and as you gear up for competitions. Image the next time you are preparing for a ride, the sound of your shoes clipping into the pedals, bodily sensations as you lean forward over the handlebars, the smells and view around you on your street. Incorporate taste as well, such as the last swallow of Gatorade. Even when conducting non-sport related tasks, begin to develop awareness of sight, hearing, touch, smell, and taste. For example, as I type these words, I can feel my wrists bent at a certain angle, and I'm aware of books, journals, etc. in my peripheral vision. I can hear the hum of the computer and am enjoying the taste of the caramel I just put in my mouth! These types of self-awareness exercises are straightforward and can be conducted throughout the day. You can gauge your initial ability levels and then try to sharpen them. By honing your awareness of not only the environment, but *yourself in the environment*, you can translate this awareness into heightened imagery for your sport and life. You will be better equipped to use bodily and environmental cues to enhance your performance.

A second tool is to compose, and then use, your own imagery script. This script could be used in training and adapted for competition. Typically, imagery use is preceded by relaxation exercises in order to clear your mind and relax your body (see Chapter 4 for more on relaxation). Try the following exercise when you can devote at least

10-15 minutes to developing your imagery. This is a short example, and we encourage you to draft your own script that can be applied in its entirety or in "sound bites" when needed. You may want to record the script, or have someone with a calm, slow-speaking voice record it for you. Longer scripts can also be devised.

This exercise can be done when you are either sitting or lying down comfortably. If sitting, place both feet on the floor, hands in your lap, and close your eyes. Think and feel all of the tension leaving your body, your shoulders dropping down, your jaw relaxed, and your head beginning to feel heavy. Let your skeleton support your muscles and take slow, deep breaths. Try to use at least a 2:4 ratio—meaning you breath in slowly and count to two and exhale twice as slowly, counting to four (with time, expand this to a count of, say, 4:8). With every breath, feel yourself melting into the chair. All of your thoughts are flowing out with each exhalation, leaving you with a clear mind. Now, pick an element of your training that you have been working to improve. Let's take the approach leading to your flip turn in the pool. Begin by feeling yourself swimming toward the wall, focusing your attention on the black line at the bottom of the pool, all parts of your body, and their coordinated movements. You are aware of the temperature of the water, the pressure of your goggles on your face, the speed you have getting closer to the wall, and the feeling of effort in your leg muscles. As you approach the wall, feel your right arm extending through the water. You can feel your arm getting through the pulling phase, and, as it reaches the end of the motion, you are aware of your mind saying, "OK, time to tuck your chin to your chest and flip your legs over as fast as possible!" We encourage you to consider all the details that go into this lead-up to the wall, remembering to use all of your senses. When the exercise is complete, do a mental review of each of your senses. Which was the easiest to conjure? (Likely sight.) Which was most difficult? (Typically smell.) Next time you try the exercise, make attempts to sharpen the other, lesser-used senses.

Imagery has the potential to shift your performance in very positive directions. It is linked to how you perceive and interpret the world and how you see yourself in action. If you can use imagery to plan out what you intend for your body to accomplish, then you are establishing goals for yourself. For example, consider the following question: Are you an analyzer or a feeler? This means if your best friends were to describe you, would they use terms like *intellectual, thinker, orderly*? Or would they use words like *dreamer, creative, emotional*? Know thyself and then work to develop the secondary perspective. If you are more of the former, this could mean you are more verbal, often thinking in words. Experiment with feelings more and incorporate your kinesthetic sense, which must be present for you to be even a mildly successful athlete. If you are more emotive, then test out use of your cognitive skills—next time you set out for a run, practice analyzing various elements of your stride, and/or integrate drills, such as fartlek training. You may also want to record these thoughts and feelings in your training logbook. It is an interesting exercise to read them over; with time, you will begin to see patterns and hopefully trace your imagery development. By recording your thoughts in general, you can become more aware of your moods, cognitions, behaviors, and how imagery may be influencing these realms. Using imagery helps to build the best machine possible by harnessing mind and body to be faster and stronger.

A few final considerations: develop strategies to deal with those less than ideal circumstances that arise during triathlons. Imaging negative events and then reversing the situation in your mind can be effective when the situation occurs. Studies have also shown that using imagery in real time is most beneficial. Ideally, you do not want to image yourself in slow motion or in fast forward, at least not for the majority of your imagery sessions. Work towards incorporating the entire event under examination into your imagery session. For instance, if you are trying to use imagery to assist you in making it through a tough hill section on the run leg, you should image the section leading up to the hill, the tough section, and then the easy part at the top of the hill. Initially you may want to image part of a sport skill to incorporate all relevant details, but your goal should be to work up to the best approximation of real time; that is, the time it would take to perform the skill physically.

CHAPTER HIGHLIGHTS

• More than 90% of Olympic athletes use imagery regularly.

• Imagery can be used in a variety of training and competitive situations.

• Consider whether you have a dominant perspective (internal or external) and whether this perspective might shift depending on the portion of your training/race.

• Incorporate the features of vividness, controllability, and emotionality into your images.

• Imagery training should be performed in a relaxed manner in a comfortable environment.

• Keep your images positive.

THE PSYCHOLOGY OF COMPETITION

SECTION II

During competition, positive PST can have significant results on performance. The first chapter in Section II considers the role of anxiety and arousal on performance and offers strategies to diminish the effect of anxiety and maximize the work done in training. The second chapter in this section examines the value of focus and concentration during competition.

4

"I DON'T KNOW WHAT HAPPENED ... I CHOKED": AROUSAL, ANXIETY, AND GENERAL STRESS DURING TRAINING AND COMPETITITON

Fear always (by definition) precedes courageous action.

K. C. Wilder

It's the night before the race and you're in bed early tossing and turning with worries about tomorrow's event circling through your mind. You wake up to the alarm, feeling less rested than you'd like, and the anxiety builds from there. You arrive at the race site, finish setting up in the transition zone, and still the butterflies won't go away. If this sounds familiar, you may need to develop some anxiety-control strategies. As the saying goes, it's not about getting rid of the butterflies, but getting them to fly in formation.

Being "stressed out" and "wound up" or "choking under pressure" refers to varying levels of combined arousal and anxiety. Although arousal and anxiety have often been used interchangeably, they have different meanings and varying effects on your sport performance. You may be asking yourself, "Does this really matter? All I know is that when I'm standing on the shore waiting for the gun to go off, I'm nervous!" Remember, as the 17th century philosopher Francis Bacon said, "Knowledge is power." The key to a successful sport psychology plan is understanding the mechanisms affecting your performance, so that you can control their influence. The following definitions are provided to gain a better understanding of the concepts covered throughout this chapter. Once you have a clear understanding of what you're dealing with, it will be less daunting. Then you can move toward relevant strategies that can be applied to training and competition.

In order to understand the relationships between anxiety and athletic performance, you need to understand some key terms. Most importantly, we need to understand the difference between arousal, which is not inherently negative, and anxiety, which is negative. The goal of this chapter is to help you recognize the signs of anxiety and to provide you with strategies to optimize (not eliminate) arousal.

Arousal refers to a dimension of intensity and can be low or high depending on your physical and emotional state. Some researchers have suggested that increased arousal is a signal that one is entering a stressful state, as evinced by physiological signs. These physiological signs can include things like increased heart rate and breathing, as well as increased perspiration and clammy hands. In general terms, being aroused means that your body and mind are preparing for activity.

Next is anxiety. Anxiety is the primary focus of this chapter, as it is potentially the most detrimental to performance. Think of anxiety as negative arousal. Richard Lazarus, a key researcher examining the role of emotion in performance, has suggested that anxiety is an emotional reaction triggered in the presence of increased cognitive processing. Anxiety occurs when individuals doubt their ability to cope with a stressful situation. It typically includes a sense of fear or impending doom regarding the outcome of the upcoming performance.

From a physiological perspective, as the body prepares for extreme exertion, one's *fight-or-flight* system takes over. The fight-or-flight system is a simple phrase to describe the human physiological reaction to stress. The human nervous system is made up of two primary divisions: the central nervous system (CNS) and the autonomic nervous system. The CNS comprises the brain, brain stem, and spinal cord. Within the autonomic system there are two branches: the sympathetic and parasympathetic systems. The sympathetic system prepares the body for activity or stress. The parasympathetic system calms us back down and brings the body back to resting state. An example might be while running, a large, growling dog suddenly appears in front of you. Your sympathetic nervous system would signal certain physiological functions; your heart rate, blood pressure, and breathing rate would increase, as would blood flow to your muscles (as you'll want to run in the other direction!). Once the potential danger has passed, your parasympathetic system would cause bodily functions to return to a calmer state. The relationship between arousal, anxiety, and performance can be charted in the following manner.

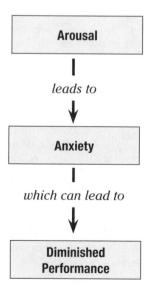

As you cluster in the starting area before hitting the water, your body likely experiences many sensations. Once the competition begins, and throughout the duration, the fight-or-flight inclination continues. Your body remains at elevated physiological levels—increased heart rate, higher blood pressure, and greater stress on your muscles, lungs, and heart.

Next, in addition to physiological changes, we need to consider whether an athlete experiences this stress rarely (say only at competitions) or whether stress is more consistent across situations. Both concepts affect training and competition. *State anxiety* is anxiety that you feel under specific situations, while *trait anxiety* is a tendency to feel greater levels of anxiety in all situations, even when the situations themselves aren't very threatening. For example, if it's normal for you to feel overly anxious only at the start of the race, this would be a state-anxiety situation. The increased anxiety in this case would be attributed to the upcoming start of the event and is not experienced in situations outside of competition. On the other hand, trait anxiety is a predisposition to perceive certain situations as threatening (for example, if you are considered to be a tense person, then you will likely experience higher anxiety levels while participating in sport, in relationships, and at work).

Regardless of whether you are a trait- or state- anxious person, anxiety can be manifested in both cognitive and physical ways. Cognitive anxiety refers to conscious awareness of unpleasant feelings, such as increased worrying and feeling overwhelmed, as well as the inability to concentrate and having difficulty making decisions. The physical (or somatic) component of anxiety involves the physiological elements such as shortness of breath and sweaty palms, as well as increases in heart rate, blood pressure, muscle tension, brain activity, breathing, and perspiration. Also, athletes frequently talk of experiencing a dry mouth and increased need to go to the bathroom. Sound familiar?

Our bodies are laboratories of sorts, and if we know what to look for, we can get a lot of useful information about our current level of functioning. There are numerous behavioral signs that indicate when you are feeling cognitive and/or physical anxiety. These include talking rapidly (or shutting down and becoming very quiet), nail biting, and rapid blinking. Think back to one of your more stressful races. As an outside observer, consider which (if any) of these cognitive, somatic, and behavioral signs you experienced consistently. Record these in the following exercise form. If you can't remember, ask a friend, training partner, or coach if they have noticed any changes in your behavior as a race approaches.

Briefly describe race experience:

_____

_____

_____

What physiological anxiety signs, if any, were you experiencing *before* the race?

_____

_____

_____

What physiological anxiety signs, if any, were you experiencing *during* the race?

_____

_____

_____

What cognitive anxiety signs, if any, were you experiencing *before* the race?

_____

_____

_____

What cognitive anxiety signs, if any, were you experiencing *during* the race?

_____

_____

_____

Once these behaviors are identified, appropriate coping strategies can be applied. Some applied sport psychologists suggest matching the strategy to the corresponding behavior. For example, if you are experiencing difficulties with negative thoughts, use one of the cognitive strategies, such as thought-stopping (a common strategy used to replace negative thoughts with positive ones). First you need to monitor your thoughts (which can be done on a daily basis, when exercising or simply walking down the street). Next, identify a random thought and determine whether it is positive or negative in orientation. For instance, "That woman is running at a faster pace than me, I am not in good shape" is inherently negative. The next step is to replace it or reword it. You could take the aforementioned thought and replace it with "Wow, look at that woman go! She'll be my inspiration for the remainder of this run!"

The relationship between anxiety and performance has been examined in endurance athletes. For instance, researchers at the University of Idaho examined pre-competitive anxiety in Ironman triathletes and found that triathletes were more cognitively and somatically anxious than either runners or cyclists. They also found that older triathletes experienced less anxiety. Something to be said for experience, perhaps?

Even more specifically, studies have examined what athletes worry about. The most frequently cited areas that athletes report feeling anxious about are their own abilities, their performance compared to others, and the dreaded *what if's*. "What if I blow a tire like in the last race?" "What if I get hit during the swim?" "What if ... ?" Consider for a moment the last time you uttered this phrase. Using imagery skills, take yourself back to that experience. Now answer the "What if ..." in a positive manner, like "What if I drop back behind some runners, recuperate, and then surge later?"

It is important to realize that some degree of elevated thinking, feeling, and physical reaction is *normal*. You've worked hard. You've swum, biked, and run many, many kilometers and are rightfully invested in your performance. Accepting that you may think, feel, and perhaps behave somewhat differently in competition compared to training reflects the fact that you care about both the process of competing and the actual result. However, increased arousal that leads to anxiety, though natural to some extent, can be detrimental to performance if it dominates your thoughts and dictates your behaviors.

There are several theories that provide explanations for how anxiety affects sport performance. The inverted-U theory suggests that individuals perform optimally at moderate levels of arousal. This relationship is presented in Figure 4.1. More specifically, if individuals are overly or under-aroused (the ends of the U shape), performance suffers. That means as an athlete, if you are too nervous, or conversely, don't care about your training/race, you are not very likely to perform to your potential.

Joseph Oxendine suggested that the inverted-U hypothesis means a slightly elevated arousal level is necessary for optimal performance on physical and cognitive tasks. He also suggested that an excessively high arousal level can interfere with performance on tasks that require fine muscle movements, coordination, and a complexity of skill. For triathletes, all three activities (swimming, cycling, and running) are considered gross motor skills (compared to sports such as archery or golf). Does this mean that anxiety is not a factor in performance in gross motor sports? Certainly not! Critics of this theory have suggested it is unidimensional and too simplistic. Also, some researchers suggest that the theory does not consider other potential factors that contribute to arousal and anxiety. However, in a broad sense, you may find some parallels with your own optimal levels of arousal linked to your best performances.

Figure 4.1: The Inverted-U Hypothesis

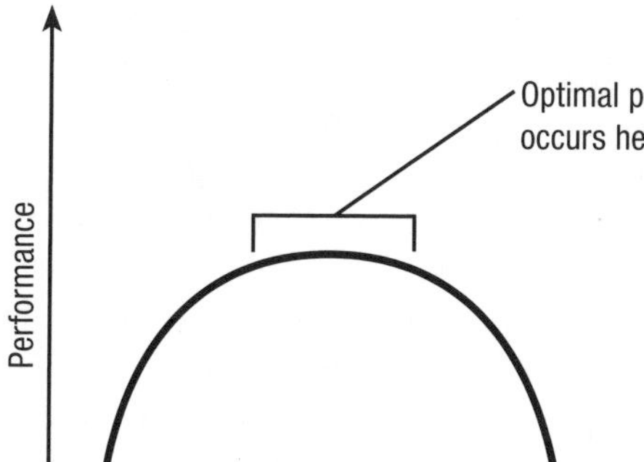

Yuri Hanin developed a theory based on the notion that each person or athlete has an individual zone of optimal functioning (or IZOF). Athletes determine their personal positive and negative feelings (Hanin uses the term "affect") when performing both optimally and poorly. The emerging pattern can then be used to predict athletes' future performances. This theory proposes that athletes can then train themselves to both recognize and move into their ideal zone of functioning.

Figure 4.2: IZOF Zones for Three Athletes (A-C)

	1 (low)		3 (mod)		5 (high)
A	Zone				
B			Zone		
C					Zone

An example of the IZOF perspective is presented in Figure 4.2. The figure shows three athletes with different zones of optimal functioning. Athlete A has been identified as working most effectively in a zone with very low levels of arousal, athlete C prefers high levels of arousal, and athlete B falls in the middle. The key is determining what level of arousal (or any emotion for that matter) will put you in that zone of optimal functioning. There is a relatively easy way to do this, however. First, think back to when you achieved your best and worst performances. Try to recall the emotions and feelings you experienced prior to those events. If this isn't possible, take a proactive approach and record the emotions and feelings you experience prior to your upcoming competitions. You should be able to see specific characteristics that reflect your zone of best performance and your zone of worst performance. Once you have figured out the characteristics that define your zone for best performance, it becomes an easy matter to use the strategies contained at the end of this chapter to create a pre-competition environment that nurtures those characteristics.

Mental Coping Strategies

Before presenting specific strategies for handling anxiety and arousal issues, there are a few important considerations worth mentioning. First, different sports require varying levels of physical arousal for optimal performance. For example, a golfer attempting a 60-foot putt will require lower physiological and psychological arousal levels than a triathlete sprinting to the finish line. Keep your specific zones of functioning in mind as you read through the following strategies.

If you've determined that you are typically over-anxious and need to relax to get into your optimal performance zone, there are ways to send messages from your muscles to your mind and vice versa. The following strategies integrate cognitive and physical forms of anxiety and will provide you with a variety of viable options.

Muscles to Mind

Breathing exercises:

Relaxation: One of the most straightforward exercises, developed by Terry Orlick, a world-renowned sport psychologist from Ottawa, Canada, involves deep breathing with two simple accompanying cues. Ideally, this exercise is performed in an area where distractions are limited, so begin by finding a quiet space. To begin, sit or lie in a comfortable position with limbs loose at your side and eyes closed. Starting with slow, deep breaths originating from your diaphragm, inhale slowly and exhale twice as slowly (e.g., inhale to the count of 3 and exhale to the count of 6). Place your hands on your abdomen, inhale through your nose, and feel your stomach expand against your palms. After the first few breaths (which will calm you physiologically) and following an exhalation, focus on relaxed fingers. After the next deep breath and slow exhalation, focus on relaxed toes. A variation of this is to simply close your eyes, take a deep breath, and exhale slowly. This easy exercise can slow the mental and physical elements of anxiety. Some people concurrently think of a calming image, such as a quiet beach at sunset. Others focus on clearing their minds and gently pushing out the anxious thoughts.

Spot check: This exercise involves becoming more familiar with specific areas in your body where muscular tension exists. Typically, the neck and shoulder region become tense as the head is the heaviest part of the body. By using a yoga-inspired exercise of sending the breath to that area, slowly rolling the head in circles or gently massaging the trapezius muscles, you can release some of the tension and increase blood flow to the area. Another spot check may be an area of the body where you've had a chronic or recurrent injury. If your knee typically flares up during runs, a gentle massage or wearing a brace may ease the tension in that area. In addition, mentally spot checking and sending the breath to that area can ease tension during training and racing. These types of exercises can be done by scanning the body during training to the point that it becomes part of your daily routine. They can also be integrated into daily stretching warm-ups and cool-downs. You will become more familiar with your tense areas and be more likely to use the strategy on race day.

A longer relaxation exercise involves sequentially tensing and relaxing muscles, beginning from the head and working to the feet. Contracting and relaxing an already tense muscle will result in a decrease in overall tension at that site.

So, let's have you try a simple relaxation exercise. To begin, get into a relaxed position and begin inhaling deeply and slowly. When feeling more relaxed, start with the muscles of your face. Scrunch up your entire face, hold for approximately five seconds, and then relax. Work from ears, neck, shoulders, arms, hands, torso, stomach, hip and glut area, thighs, knees, shins down to the feet, and finally the toes. Compare the overall body sensation you had before you began the exercise and note the warm, relaxed feelings at the end of the exercise.

Stretching:
Stretching is another effective way to relieve both physical and mental tension. Although most athletes are taught the benefits of stretching, many rush through short pre-training stretches without getting the full benefits. Ideally, even on off-training days, athletes should complete a stretching routine with both general and sport-specific stretches. This increases circulation, enhances flexibility and mobility, and decreases the risk of injury. All stretches should be done following a 10-15 minute cardiovascular warm-up to increase blood flow. Stretches should be held for at least 15 seconds without pulsing or bouncing. Gently pushing the muscles to lengthen without pain is important. Consult a coach or a training manual for specific stretches and then incorporate these into your daily training regime.

Massage:
Receiving a massage from a trained massage therapist or masseuse can be a very relaxing, refreshing experience. Similar to stretching, the

manipulations increase the flow of oxygen to muscles. With massage, deeper muscle tissues can be exploited, which can do wonders for flexibility and recovery.

Mind to Muscle

Part of coping with stress and anxiety depends on how you appraise the situation. Controlling thought processes can greatly influence performance. Some strategies for controlling anxiety using the mind are presented below.

Imagery:

Imagery was the focus of Chapter 3. However, with regard to anxiety, it is important to note that in addition to using all of your senses, it is worthwhile to incorporate relevant emotions (such as feeling anxious) in creating the image. Many athletes use imagery on race day, but neglect to include the accompanying emotions. For example, are you keyed up or preoccupied with the fact you forgot your favorite singlet? If so, how can you use one of the mental strategies in this chapter (or other chapters) to deal with this tension, and race to your potential?

Thought-stopping and self-talk:

A primary area of anxiety control is thought-stopping. As demonstrated in a previous example in this chapter, thought-stopping entails first recognizing what you are saying to yourself and determining whether these thoughts are negative or detrimental. What is the voice in your head telling you? We will also discuss the concept of *self-talk* to a greater extent in the next chapter.

Race plan development:

Having a plan for race day can have a positive effect on controlling anxiety. This preparation should begin weeks in advance and include such factors as having your bike checked, deciding what shorts/singlet you'll wear, how you will get to the venue, what food you'll bring, etc. Depending on your level of organization, you should be able to determine how much planning is required for an organized race day that is void of anxiety. Writing down the specifics of this plan in your log can help hold you accountable and allow you to rework the plan clearly if needed (e.g., if a race start time is delayed).

Control the controllables:
This is a simple cognitive strategy. Let's say you wake up early on a Saturday morning, looking forward to a tough brick workout, and it's pouring rain. The weather is not under your control (neither, for that matter, are your competitors, lousy officials, etc.) However, your attitude and adoption of anxiety-control strategies are under your control. Recognizing this, and keeping your mind focused on what you can control (e.g., using thought-stopping techniques) can have positive effects on your performance.

Meditation and yoga:
Meditation and yoga are gaining more mainstream popularity as practices to decrease stress and anxiety and as healthy ways to simplify and prioritize one's life. These activities entail achieving a mental equilibrium and a calming of the mind and body. Meditation and yoga are both mind-to-muscle and muscle-to-mind exercises. Elements of awareness and insight are incorporated into looking inward, reflection on the self and the present moment. This simple and pure approach can be attained through the practice of various forms of yoga.

Energizing

Sometimes athletes, due to stress or generally low arousal levels, could benefit from techniques that *increase* their arousal level. This can be managed by staying expressive and paying attention to what you are feeling. By doing this you can use self-talk and assertive statements to prepare for training and competition. "I WILL charge the last mile of the run!" would be an example of a strong, empowering self-talk statement. Music can serve as an excellent motivator; some athletes chose to make

Great occasions do not make heroes or cowards; they simply unveil them to the eyes of men. Silently and imperceptibly, as we wake or sleep, we grow strong or weak, and at last some crisis shows what we have become.

Brooke Foss Westcott

a personal tape or CD that they can listen to leading up to the start of the race. Another method used by athletes is a highlight video, which, with the help of training partners and/or coaches, can be made from performances throughout the year. Ideally, the tape contains images of you successfully training and racing, in good form and in positive spirits. The tape can have your favorite upbeat music playing along with the images, making the video useful on days when you're feeling down and need extra energy.

In summary, being physically and psychologically aroused for training and competition is the ideal performance state. However, it is normal for athletes to experience varying levels of arousal, which can lead to anxiety. Although there are a variety of theoretical rationales for the development of anxiety, athletes will likely gain more from focusing on applied exercises to manage anxiety. The examples provided in this chapter will aid you in recognizing and coping with anxiety in all elements of your triathlon preparation.

CHAPTER HIGHLIGHTS

• Arousal is a direction of intensity and is not inherently negative.

• Unmanaged anxiety can have a significant effect on your performance.

• Psychological and physiological cues can be used to evaluate anxiety levels.

• Determine your specific optimal level of functioning and use mental skills training to recreate this state when needed.

• Muscle-to-mind activities such as stretching, deep breathing, and massage can be used to reduce anxiety.

• Mind-to-muscle activities such as imagery, thought-stopping, planning, and meditation are also effective for managing anxiety.

5

KEEPING YOUR HEAD IN THE RACE: FOCUS AND CONCENTRATION

Sometimes you have an idea of how you want a race to go, what you want to get out of it, and how you want to place. In my case, I want to win the whole thing. Ironman is always a thousand times more than you could ever imagine. When you feel good about your performance, then the feeling is great. When you do poorly, that too can really be magnified in yourself.

Mark Allen

Triathletes spend countless hours and dollars making sure that their bikes are ready for race day. Then they take time to find the best spot in transition to shave precious seconds from their finishing time. Much thought is given to ensuring that equipment and set-up are optimal for performance, but what about achieving optimal mental focus on race day? Maintaining concentration and focus during competition is important to triathletes at all levels of competition. Focus on relevant stimuli during competition can often make the difference between winning, setting a personal best, and achieving less desirable outcomes. While focus during competition may seem like a rather straightforward concept, in actuality it has many facets. This chapter will explore focus and concentration as they pertain to triathlon training and competition.

Cognitive Orientation

Sport psychologists have known for quite some time that the mind plays an enormous role in determining whether you have the race of your life or one you wish you could forget. For example, what do you think about during a triathlon? Some triathletes (as well as many athletes from other sports) discount the power of their thoughts. But research indicates that the thoughts that you have during competition can have a dramatic impact on your sport performance.

The way that you think during a race usually fits into one of two categories: thoughts that are *associative* or thoughts that are *dissociative*. Associative thoughts center on how the body is performing during the event. They include focusing on pacing, form, or strategy. Conversely, dissociative thoughts are almost hypnotic, as they require cutting off from what is going on around you. When an athlete concentrates on singing a song in their head or noticing the scenery going by, they are dissociating from the physiological information that their body is trying to provide. There has been a significant amount of research done on the beneficial effects of both associative and dissociative coping skills in endurance sports. Determining which coping strategy is the most appropriate for you really depends on numerous factors, including your racing goals, the strategy you adopt naturally, and the strategy that has worked for you in

the past. Here are some suggestions, but it is always best to try different strategies to determine which one fits your needs best.

Competitive—If you are a competitive triathlete, you probably want to focus on using associative thinking processes as much as possible during your races. Research done with marathon runners indicates that athletes who spend a greater amount of time associating during competition run faster than runners who use dissociative thought processes. By associating with the physical processes that are going on during the event, you can better prepare to address problems such as pacing, dehydration, and pain.

Middle of the pack—If you are a middle-of-the-pack triathlete, the coping strategy you use depends on how comfortable you are with your current level of performance. If you are at a plateau and are interested in becoming faster or more competitive, then you should try to incorporate more associative coping strategies into your racing. If you don't get to train as much as you like and are comfortable finishing in the middle of the pack and/or race purely for enjoyment, dissociative strategies are likely the way to go.

Survival—If you are doing your first triathlon or increasing your race distance, and are just concerned with surviving, dissociation may be most helpful. Dissociation will provide you with essential distractions you may need to take your mind off the prolonged discomfort connected to racing longer distances.

Even if you are an elite triathlete, the chances of you being able to use associative coping strategies during an entire triathlon are highly unlikely. Regardless of your athletic level or concentration skills, it is increasingly difficult to maintain focus for extended lengths of time. The longer the race, the more difficult this becomes. Don't become frustrated or discouraged when your mind starts to wander. This will happen. However, try to restrict its wandering to periods when you can afford it. This may be in the middle of the bike leg, or during the mid-section of the run. But, bring your focus back to the race when the need arises. For example, during the later stages of the run leg when pacing and fatigue start to interfere with performance, there is a greater need to stay focused on your physical condition.

Examples of associative strategies include

1. Focusing on form. Focusing on the mechanics of maintaining an efficient swim or pedal stroke are associative thoughts.

2. Keeping non-essential muscles relaxed. When non-essential muscles are tense, you waste energy. Concentrating on keeping your shoulders relaxed during the run or keeping your neck less tense during the bike are examples of relaxing non-essential muscles.

3. Being aware of your heart rate. Change in heart rate can be a good indicator of possible upcoming problems due to energy depletion, dehydration, or pushing your body too hard.

Now, up to this point, dissociation has been presented in a negative light. Dissociation is not a bad thing. In fact, it can be very useful and has saved a number of triathletes from the dreaded Did Not Finish (DNF). Cutting yourself off from feelings of discomfort or boredom is where dissociation is helpful. For example, the next time you start to feel saddle sore or bored, try to dissociate from the discomfort of the situation. Here are some possible ways to do this:

1. Counting. Count the number of telephone poles, fire hydrants, phone booths, anything.

2. Mental Mathematics. Choose a number and divide it by 7 or multiply it by 11. Experiment. Some athletes use mental music—singing a favorite song to themselves.

3. Scenery. Take it in. Enjoy the beauty and fresh air of your surroundings.

4. Instant Wealth. Go over in your mind what you would do if you were instantly wealthy. What would be the first thing you would buy?

5. Problem Solving. Consider a challenge in your life. Pick one that is not overly distressing, but one where the pros/cons involved can be considered objectively.

The key to these dissociation exercises is to occupy your mind with irrelevant thoughts, thereby filling attentional space that, left unfilled, could become focused on feelings of discomfort and soreness. However, there is a fine line between discomfort and pain from the onset of a possible injury. Common sense, patience, and experience will help you distinguish the two. Overall, you have options regarding the use of associative and/or dissociative strategies. If you believe you are able to control your thoughts on a consistent basis, you are on your way to being able to monitor, and positively influence your performance.

> *The greatest discovery of my generation is that human beings can alter their lives by altering their attitudes of mind.*
>
> **William James**

Self-Talk

We've referred to cognitions and thought-stopping previously in this book. This section will further elaborate. Self-talk refers to the internal monologue that each of us have with ourselves (that is, it's that little voice we hear in our head). As you may have experienced, this little voice becomes increasingly important during competition. Consider the following statements from two triathletes encountering a difficult hill on the run course.

1. "Is this hill ever going to end? I feel like my heart is going to explode."

2. "I am tired but so is everyone else. If I dig deep I could really put distance on some of the people behind me."

If these two athletes had the same physical capabilities, which one do you think would reach the top of the hill first? The statement by the first athlete is extremely negative. It's common to experience some self-doubt, or to have negative thoughts creep in during training or competition. It's how you handle these types of thoughts that will determine whether your performance is undermined. Negative thoughts can lead to a pessimistic self-evaluation, which has the potential to influence future performances. On the other hand, focusing on positive, affirming thoughts has the ability to create a sense of euphoria, empowerment, and a strong belief in one's self.

Still not convinced? Try this test. When you get up tomorrow morning, let the first words out of your mouth be "I feel fantastic. This is going to be an amazing day." But saying these words is not enough—you have to make a deliberate and conscious effort to believe that you feel fantastic. When people greet you in the morning and ask how you are doing, reply that you are "fantastic." At lunchtime, try the opposite. Repeat out loud "I feel crappy. I can't wait for this day to be over" and focus on these thoughts for the entire afternoon. How did your different foci affect your attitude, productivity, and interactions with others throughout the day?

Now apply these principles to your race situations. There are always mishaps that will occur during competition. Examples include tire punctures, wrong turns, or missing a drink at an aid station. Everyone faces these obstacles at some point. However, the effect that these incidents have on your overall result is largely determined by your attitude. John Hellemans, a triathlon coach and author from New Zealand, writes, "the more positive and constructive the response, the less likely it is to affect overall performance." Start thinking of mishaps as opportunities rather than obstacles. For example, you could perceive a three-minute penalty for drafting on the Ironman bike course as three minutes of well-deserved rest. If you focus on the negative and see it as an additional three minutes to your finishing time, it will likely cost you even greater time due to the negativity you will take with you on the run course. Monumental sporting events, such as Roger Banister breaking the four-minute mile, would never have been possible without focusing on positive outcomes.

The specific content of the self-talk statements is also important. Bill Rodgers, five-time winner of the Boston Marathon, is an excellent practitioner of positive self-talk. During his extraordinary racing career, he would usually let others lead until the later stages of the race, at which point he took, and usually kept, the lead. Prior to making his move, Rodgers would think, "Look out. Once I grab the lead I'm going to really be running well, and you're going to have to kill yourself to catch me." Note the positive qualities of his statement. Also important is that Rodgers provided an outlet from the situation if things did not go his way. He did not say, "I am going to take the lead late in the race, and no one is going to be able to pass me." Such a rigid statement would leave no room for compromise in the event that things did not go his way, and anything less than a victory may be viewed as failure. Rodgers' actual statement allowed for a possible mental exit from the situation without the athlete manifesting feelings of failure. Rodgers' statement does not say that no one is going to pass him once he takes the lead or that he is going to win the race. He indirectly states that passing him is possible, but that the athlete passing him will have to "kill himself" to do it.

It's important to provide an indirect mental exit from the situation when using self-talk, should the unthinkable happen and you don't reach your goals. By providing an indirect exit from the situation you have not placed your entire self-concept on the line if you don't succeed. It is also important to note Rodgers' use of "I" at the beginning of the statement. It indicates focusing on personal performance and capabilities rather than competitors.

Another important consideration is that self-talk is very individualized. The positive internal monologue that your training partner has will not necessarily work for you. Personalize thoughts and phrases during competition so that they are specifically beneficial to you. Through experimentation in training and racing you can refine a self-talk system that works best for you. Remember, where the mind leads, the body will follow.

Perfecting Your Self-Talk

At your next strenuous workout (or competition), keep a mental list of the types of things you are saying to yourself. Record these thoughts on the chart below. Once you've created a list of self-talk statements, rate whether they are positive or negative. Use the information in the above section to transform your negative self-talk statements into positive statements.

Self-Talk Statement	Rating (P or N)	Transformation

Let me tell you the secret that has led me to my goal. My strength lies solely in my tenacity.

Louis Pasteur

Cue Words

As discussed in the previous section, the words we use have a tremendous affect on our mental state and thereby our physical performance. Maintaining a positive mental focus can be as simple as identifying a few cue words that have powerful, positive meanings to you. The use of cue words has wide application in the world of sport. Anyone from baseball pitchers to sprinters can use cue words to relax during periods of intense competition anxiety. However, the use of cue words is not limited to situations that produce anxiety. For triathlon competition in particular, they have a variety of uses.

It is amazing how much cognitive information can be stored in a single word. For example, the word "relax" could have various meanings to different athletes. "Relax" could serve as a reminder to remove tension from the shoulders, lengthen the running stride, forget external factors such as work or family problems, and/or maintain a useful breathing rhythm. Other words such as "energize" or "fuel up" could be used at a low point in a race to raise spirits and create a positive mental state. For you, the key is to identify the specific words that have the most personal meaning. It is important to use these words in training, so that when you need to rely on them during competition, your response will be almost second nature.

Developing, practicing, and applying cue words: To begin, simply increase your awareness of thoughts that are automatic during training and/or competition. Note mentally (or even in a training log) what words or statements come naturally to mind while you are working out. These words can then be applied to areas in your race performance that require improvement in attentional focus. These problem areas may include maintaining focus during your least favorite segment, running shoulder to shoulder with another competitor at a challenging pace, or refocusing attention after changing to the bike or run leg. Try to identify the areas where your performance breaks down or you notice a change in your thought patterns.

The next step is to try to identify what it is that causes these breakdowns and use cue words that will accommodate these problems.

Are these changes in your thoughts and/or performance usually caused by physical or mental fatigue? If this is the case, try using cue words like "focus" or "intense" to bring your focus back to the present situation. If the performance breakdown is due to low energy levels, then there are other considerations besides simply refocusing attention. Don't panic, ingest some food and fluids, and use key words like "energy" and "power" to raise your spirits so that you will be ready to capitalize on this fuel when it is metabolized. Certainly there are going to be situations that arise in competition that will be specific to your unique circumstances and race history. For instance, in a particularly challenging hill on the bike leg, your focus may be sharpened by repeating an energizing key word (e.g., "power" or "strong") either in your head or out loud. These words serve as affirmations, descriptions of a desired situation.

Remember that cue words and affirmations, like self-talk, are highly individualized. The words that work for someone else may not be the most effective words for you. Experiment with different words and pick the ones that work best. Review your best-ever sport (and life!) performances. Invest in a thesaurus if need be. Place the cue words where you can see them. Kevin Mackinnon, one of Canada's top triathlon coaches, suggests placing the words on your bike stem where you'll be able to see them. This simple exercise could make a world of difference.

CHAPTER SUMMARY

• Proper focus can have a significant influence on performance.

• Associative thoughts are linked to higher levels of performance.

• Dissociative thoughts are useful for dealing with discomfort and boredom.

• Negative self-talk can undermine your performance. Make sure that the little voice in your head is staying positive.

• Use 'cue words' during difficult times to stay focused on the task at hand.

• Use a journal or training log to record thoughts and feelings ... hold yourself accountable.

OTHER ISSUES

SECTION III

In addition to psychological issues during training and competition, other important factors can have a significant effect on your ability to train and race at your potential. The first chapter in this section considers the role of psychology in preventing and recovering from injuries. This is followed by a discussion of the value of reflection and self-awareness in maximizing your triathlon involvement. The final chapter provides tips to assist you in sticking with your new mental training program.

6

WHEN DISASTER STRIKES: DEALING WITH PAIN AND INJURIES

If I had a formula for bypassing trouble, I wouldn't pass it around. Wouldn't be doing anybody a favor. Trouble creates a capacity to handle it. I don't say embrace trouble. That's as bad as treating it as an enemy. But I do say, meet it as a friend, for you'll see a lot of it and had better be on speaking terms with it.
Oliver Wendell Holmes

Due to the extreme amount of training that is required for participation in triathlons, regardless of the length, training-related injuries are a common occurrence. This was a consistent finding from our study of Ironman triathletes. However, even though injuries are common, one of the most difficult things for athletes to do is to stop training long enough for the injury to heal. Taking time away from training is often seen as unproductive. However, not taking the time to recover sufficiently from an injury can lead to chronic problems with performance and the possibility of long-term health loss. In order to recover from an injury, the body requires a specific amount of time to physiologically heal damaged tissues. Research has indicated that providing an optimal mental climate for healing can decrease the amount of recovery time required before returning to normal training. In this chapter, we examine the psychological basis for many injuries and provide useful techniques to facilitate a return to normal training. In addition, we discuss staleness, overtraining, and burnout, problems that are especially relevant to triathletes.

> *There are risks and costs to action. But they are far less than the long-range risks of comfortable inaction.*
> **John F. Kennedy**

Stress and Injuries

From a psychological standpoint, there are a number of factors contributing to injury, the most influential factor being psychological stress. Psychological stress is distinguishable from the physiological stress necessary for training adaptations. Psychological stress can take many forms. For example, if an athlete finds a particular competition especially threatening, his or her stress may rise, which can then increase the incidence of injury. As we have highlighted throughout this book, athletes are unique and, therefore, the circumstances that increase stress for one athlete will not necessary increase stress levels for another athlete. Consequently, it is useful to identify the factors or situations that increase *your* stress levels. Some things to consider are as follows:

> Presence of significant others—Are you affected by the presence or absence of significant others, such as spouses, friends, and family among the race spectators? Do you feel an increased pressure to perform well when significant others are in the crowd?

> Presence of key competitors—How are you affected by having to race against your key competitors and/or training partners? Do these circumstances lead to an increased psychological burden during the race? Do you feel supported? Are you confused by these feelings—that people are supporting you and yet you still feel nervous?

Racing on courses associated with negative experiences—How are you affected by places where you had less than optimal performances? How are you affected by courses that have a challenging reputation (e.g., racing in the Hawaiian heat in your first Ironman World Championships)?

The items provided above are only a few of the possible stressors that can contribute to getting and sustaining an injury. Further, the most salient stressors are often ones that are not related to triathlon competition at all, such as problems with work or family relationships. It is important to consider how stressful events affect you, and then develop methods of neutralizing these effects.

One of the major theories used to examine sports injuries is the *attentional disruption theory*. This theory suggests that stress interferes with an athlete's peripheral attention, and that this affects the athlete's ability to respond to relevant environmental stimuli. For example, during a cross-country run, reduced peripheral attention could interfere with proper foot placement, resulting in a turned ankle. Now consider the range of environmental cues you must consider during each of the events of the triathlon—things such as avoiding other swimmers' arms and legs, pedestrians and volunteers on the bike course, loose gravel on corners and turn-arounds, inattentive traffic directors, etc. The list is overwhelming. Although there are many internal and external stimuli during a race like the triathlon, there is no time for decreased attention.

There has also been speculation that adopting a dissociative orientation during competition and training can lead to increased incidences of injury (recall the chapter on Focus and Concentration). The logic of this argument is as follows: when you do not attend to internal stimuli (i.e., association), and instead use distraction and other dissociative foci, you will not be aware of subtle signs, such as tightness and/or pain, that can signal the onset of an injury. While this argument seems logical, it hasn't received strong support from research.

Slogans used in North American society can also have negative influences on athletes' susceptibility to injury. Slogans such as "ride hard or ride home alone" or "no pain, no gain" can influence athletes to push themselves beyond their limits, consequently increasing injury rates. It is important to pay attention to the psychological orientation you use during training and racing—it could be an important factor in reducing your chance of injury. Instead of adopting mental attitudes that regard pain as something that can *always* be pushed through and overcome, focus on pain as being what it is, the body's signal that you are pushing too hard. Instead of slogans like "no pain, no gain," adopt slogans like "train hard and smart" or "quality over quantity." These slogans reflect a safer training focus, and research has indicated that changing your focus in this manner can reduce incidences of injury.

While it is imperative to pay attention to feelings of pain during training, for the triathlete this is not always easy to do. Pushing physiological limits is uncomfortable. Therefore, the ability to distinguish between discomfort and pain becomes important. The discomfort associated with pushing hard during training (i.e., during intervals, hill climbs) is beneficial to performance, while physical pain is (obviously) detrimental to performance. Experience will best teach you how to distinguish one from the other. However, being attentive and aware is always to your benefit. In general, this mindset will help you to better know your body's capacities and limits.

> *Nothing in life just happens. It isn't enough to believe in something. ... You have to have stamina ... to struggle ... to meet obstacles and overcome them.*
>
> **Golda Meir**

Overtraining, Staleness, and Burnout

Ever been really tired, despite a clean bill of health? Ever found yourself lacking motivation to train for an extended period of time? While most endurance athletes have heard of the terms *overtraining, staleness,* and *burnout,* most cannot distinguish them from each other. This isn't surprising, given there is little agreement even among researchers as to the meaning of each specific term. Therefore, before we go any further, let's outline our working definitions of these terms to avoid any misunderstandings along the way.

Jeurgen Froehlich is a successful masters swimmer, physician, and researcher investigating overtraining in endurance athletes. According to Froehlich, *overtraining* refers to forms of training that lead to *overtraining syndrome*—a period of decreased performance and profound feelings of fatigue. *Staleness,* on the other hand, refers to either the initial response to overtraining or a prolonged period of overtraining lasting several weeks. Overtraining that is not corrected can lead to the state of physical and mental exhaustion known as *burnout*. Triathletes at all levels need to develop and maintain awareness relative to overtraining and burnout. Staleness is a precursor to these states … a potential warning sign. You can use Table 6.1 to assess any signs you may have noted in yourself, past or present. Consider a time when you think you might have been overtraining. Now circle each sign that you were experiencing. This chapter will help you to not only recognize, but deal with these signs should you experience them in the future.

Table 6.1: Physiological and Psychological Signs and Symptoms of Overtraining Syndrome

Physiological Signs

Decreased performance	Changes in heart rate at rest, exercise, and recovery
Inability to meet previously attained performance standards	Increased frequency of respiration
Recovery is prolonged	Increased perspiration
Reduced toleration of training load	Decreased body fat
Decreased muscular strength	Chronic fatigue
Decreased work capacity	Insomnia
Loss of coordination	Thirst
Decreased efficiency or decreased amplitude of movement	Loss of appetite
	Headaches
Reappearance of mistakes already corrected	Nausea
Reduced capacity of differentiation and correcting technical faults	Increased aches and pains
	Muscle soreness and tenderness
Increased difference between lying and standing heart rate	Gastrointestinal disturbances
	Muscle damage

Psychological Signs

Feelings of depression	Fear of competition
General apathy	Changes in personality
Decreased self-esteem or worsening feelings of self	Decreased ability to narrow concentration
Emotional instability	Increased distractibility
Difficulty concentrating at work and training	Decreased capacity to deal with large amounts of information
Sensitive to environmental and emotional stress	Decreased determination in tough situations

Symptoms of Overtraining Syndrome

The feelings and symptoms associated with overtraining syndrome are as varied as the athletes reporting them. Table 6.1 presents a list of the physiological and psychological symptoms that are easiest to recognize without the need for lab tests and blood work. However, researchers have also identified a number of biochemical and immunological markers to diagnose overtraining syndrome. Interestingly, for some athletes several symptoms must be present for them to experience overtraining syndrome, while for other athletes a single symptom is enough. Without losing faith, athletes can learn to detect their own warning signs.

Overtraining syndrome is most common in sports that require progressive training loads to promote the adaptations necessary for performance improvement. Therefore, endurance and ultra-endurance sports—such as swimming, running, cycling, and triathlon—are prime candidates. To better understand overtraining syndrome and its prevention, it is necessary to understand the physiological mechanisms that are involved.

Promoting Positive Training Adaptations

Our understanding of the relationship between training stress and adaptation (e.g., improved performance) is derived from Hans Selye's General Adaptation Syndrome. Selye's research is based on the concept that the body has a three-stage response to stress: shock/alarm, adaptation/resistance, and staleness/exhaustion.

In triathlon the shock/alarm phase is distinguished by the acute muscle soreness and performance decreases associated with the onset of a new or different training stimulus. During this stage, the body is moved out of homeostasis (i.e., its normal range of functioning) and must adapt to the new levels of stress. During the adaptation/resistance stage, the body adapts to the training stimuli and regains homeostatic function. These adaptations may be positive, as in a reorganization of functional mechanisms to produce a superior, more capable operating system. They may also be negative, such as in the occurrence of a physical injury or mental overload. In the staleness/exhaustion stage, physiological adaptations are typically no longer being made and performance may again decrease unless training stimuli are modified. During this stage, the athlete has adapted to the previous level of physical or mental stress, and training at this level no longer disrupts homeostasis to the same extent.

The duration of the period from shock to staleness is determined primarily by the intensity of the initial training stressor (stage one). Higher levels of stress require more time to achieve adaptation. If the time between adaptation and new training is too long, maximal training effects are compromised. On the other hand, if the time is too short, coaches and athletes run the risk of incurring injuries or overtraining syndrome.

In order to meet the ideal stressor-adaptation balance, athletes and coaches use a concept called *periodization*. Over the past two decades, this concept has become increasingly important to the year-long development of endurance athletes. The Oxford Dictionary of Sports Science and Medicine defines the term periodization as the "organization of a training year into different periods to attain different objectives." The purpose of using periodization to design training programs  is to allow the athlete to attend to useful training objectives during early periods of the training year while maintaining an optimal level of readiness during the competitive season.

The periodization model is rooted in the notion that periods of high training stress should be alternated with periods of relatively low training stress to allow for maximal adaptation with minimal risk of overtraining or overuse injuries. This is achieved by dividing an athlete's training year into different phases of training. For example, a training year may be made up of four phases: preparation, pre-competition, competition, and recovery. The length of each phase varies with recovery (i.e., the off-season) typically being the shortest and preparation typically being the longest. The focus of each phase is determined by its position relative to upcoming competitions. For instance, the recovery phase would likely occur immediately following the end of the competitive season and would be followed by a training cycle focusing on physical preparation for the next year's competitive season. Also, recovery needs to take place between competitions, providing the body and mind time to recuperate. To tie this back to our discussion of the stages of adaptation, periodization of training is intended to prevent athletes from spending too much time in the third stage (staleness/exhaustion) by varying training schedules, so that new training stimuli are presented at the end of the adaptation phase.

Acute Injuries

Up until this point, we have focused on injuries that are the result of training imbalances or stress, but unfortunately these factors aren't the only source for injuries. Ballistic injuries from bike crashes or falls during running are also a common occurrence. These sorts of acute injuries can wreak havoc not only with our systematic approach to training, but also to our sense of psychological well-being. Imagine how your psychological state would be affected if you had trained for the past year for a key triathlon competition, only to suffer a bike accident in the weeks leading up the race. Having a set of strategies to deal with this situation can not only make it more bearable to experience, but will get you back into your normal training routine faster.

The benefits of mental training using imagery and visualization are presented in an earlier chapter (Chapter 3), but they are equally relevant for the management of sports injuries. A number of areas related to injury are examined below, accompanied by psychological strategies for enhanced recovery.

Continuity of Physical and Mental Training

It is rare that an athlete will have the sort of injury that will necessitate a total break from training. Therefore, it is important to maintain training continuity in those areas where you can still train. For example, a knee injury may mean time away from the pounding of running, but swimming is still a viable option. If the injury is so severe that even swimming is too strenuous, there is still upper body weight training. All attempts should be made to maintain (and even enhance!) your current level of physiological conditioning. This will facilitate a more rapid return to pre-injury training levels, as well as increase self-confidence and self-efficacy.

Moreover, regardless of the extent of your injury, you are still able to attend to the mental aspects of sport performance. Continued mental practice on those skills outlined in previous sections of this book will help you to maintain your competitive mindset. If you haven't been spending the required amounts of time developing your arsenal of mental strategies, this may be the perfect time to develop those abilities. At least keep your head in the game if your body must sit out! Attend group swim and run workouts and project yourself into the performance situation. Mentally rehearse key portions of your competitions so that you maintain or develop the ideal performance state.

Using Imagery to Facilitate Healing

Research examining the role that a psychological state can have on rates of healing suggests that adopting a positive mental state is beneficial to recovery. It may be that the positive mental state is actually enhancing recovery or it may serve to decrease injury-induced anxiety. At any rate, imagery should be considered when dealing with injuries.

Athletes should be cognizant of the focus of their images. Focusing on the incidents that lead to the injury has been found to have a negative effect on recovery. This is particularly true if an athlete is fearful of re-injury. Instead focus on positive images that will aid in the healing process. These can include images of the healing process or the injury being healed and fully functional. John Heil, a psychologist who specializes in sports injuries, suggests using imagery with the following physical remedies:

• Image that the application of ice to the injured area freezes up and shuts down pain receptors.

• Image that medications (e.g., anti-inflammatory agents) act as sponges to absorb local tissue irritants.

• Image that deep breathing infuses the body with energy to release endorphins and aid recovery.

• During rehab, image blood flowing to the muscle and rebuilding damaged tissue at an accelerated rate.

• Image your ligaments as wound steel and rubber-strong but flexible.

• Image the spinal column supported by tendon, ligament, and muscle, like the rigging of a great sailing ship.

• Create images that are most effective for you and your sport situation.

Dealing with Pain

Mental strategies are also effective in dealing with the pain associated with an injury. In Chapter 5 we discussed how cognitive orientation could moderate feelings of discomfort or fatigue. Similar strategies can be applied to managing pain. The good news is that athletes are generally better at dealing with pain than non-athletes. Dennis Turk  and his colleagues identified a number of methods for dealing with injury pain. The first method is called *external focus of attention* and involves simply directing your attention away from feelings of pain and toward things that are happening in your environment. For example, watching an engaging movie or television program will provide a temporary distraction. *Pleasant imagining* is another possible coping strategy. This strategy involves focusing your attention on internal thoughts that are pleasant. Pleasant images will differ from one individual to the next, but thoughts of relaxing on a sunny beach or sharing a meal with a significant other will likely produce feelings of pleasantness and decreased feelings of pain for most individuals. A similar strategy is *neutral imagining*. This involves focusing on neutral events or tasks such as the mechanics of walking up a flight of stairs or shuffling a deck of cards. Performing a *rhythmic cognitive activity* has also been found to be effective in coping with pain. When using this method, athletes devote their attention to performing a repetitive mental task such as counting from 1 to 100 or repeating a mantra over and over. *Dramatized coping* involves associating the pain with higher order purposes or heroic deeds. Imagining that the pain is a result of superior athletic output or accomplishment is an example. The final strategy that Turk presents is *pain acknowledging*. This strategy is a bit different than the others in that it requires athletes to focus on the pain itself and to try to disassociate the pain from the injury. For example, during this strategy, you would focus on the sensation of the pain and try to discern the specific neurological signals that are coming from the injury to your brain. The purpose of this strategy is to try to develop the ability to make neurological signals slow down or become less powerful.

Fear of Re-Injury

The fear of re-injury can often be as debilitating as the injury itself. Reassure yourself that it's normal to feel fear or self-doubt at the prospect of performing activities similar to those that initially caused your injury. Humans are creatures of habit, and the most significant learning we do comes from trial and error. Our minds and bodies are naturally wired to feel fear and apprehension when performing activities we know can be harmful. The key to managing fear is to recognize that fear is just another element of performance to be managed. However, if fear and apprehension are not managed correctly, they can lead to anxiety and/or stress, and potential association problems. Using strategies such as self-talk, relaxation, and anxiety control can aid in managing fear of re-injury.

Be Aware of Negative Self-Talk

It is also important to be aware of your inner dialogue when dealing with an injury and to recognize that you are not immune to negative thoughts about yourself. For example, injured athletes commonly experience negative thoughts such as "It isn't fair that others get to compete and I can't." The essential thing is to recognize these thoughts and be aware of their effect on your mood and ultimately your behavior. Use the strategies we discussed in Chapter 5 to change your perspective from negative to positive. Many athletes find it more helpful to view their injury as a challenge to overcome, which will help them develop into stronger athletes and people.

The key to dealing with an injury is first recognizing that these things happen and that it has happened to you. Once you've resigned yourself to the fact that you're injured, you can begin to take the appropriate steps to recovery and return to triathlon better than ever.

Accept that some days you're the pigeon, and some days you're the statue.

Anonymous

CHAPTER HIGHLIGHTS

• Injuries are a normal part of training, but using psychological training can minimize their influence on your fitness.

• An optimal psychological outlook can facilitate healing and recovery.

• Psychological stress can predispose you to an increased risk of injury.

• Be aware of the psychological and physiological signs of overtraining syndrome.

• Use periodization to balance the stress of training with adequate recovery.

• Use visualization and imagery to continue training during injury.

• Psychological skills can be used to manage the pain and discomfort associated with an injury.

"HOW DID I PERFORM?": USING REFLECTION TO BECOME ANALYTIC AND STRATEGIC[1]

The weekly tune-ups ... teach you how far you can go. If you perform poorly, you have a chance to redeem yourself the next week. The big deals, like Ironman, demand consistency, commitment, patience, and preparation. You invest in that goal every single day of the year. The mental and physical effort, the highs and the lows, are all seeds that you plant along the way. Race day is harvest time; that's when you reap the benefits.

Mark Allen

A consistent finding from performance literature is that athletes in all sports and at all performance levels can become better able to contribute to their own performance, whatever their ultimate goal. One method is through reflection on performance. Using existing knowledge and feedback from previous performances and the individuals in your training group, you can enhance performance by employing mental processes (e.g., reflection). By now, the concept of reflection should

be familiar. It is an essential component of an effective goal-setting program. However, we feel that reflection is valuable enough to warrant a chapter of its own.

Successful performers in sports and other domains approach tasks with confidence, diligence, and resourcefulness. These qualities are not purely the result of greater knowledge or more refined physical capabilities. Expert performers also have the ability to implement appropriate regulatory strategies to analyze, review, interpret, plan, and subsequently intervene to assist their performance during competition. Regardless of the domain, expert performers are often described as being self-critical, displaying instances of reflection, control, and 'playfulness.' Elite athletes are aware of the knowledge and skills they possess as well as their areas of weakness, and they ultimately use viable means to 1) implement useful strategies to emphasize skills they possess and 2) acquire skills they lack. As a result, they are able to overcome weaknesses. Expert athletes reflect on past performances to devise methods to improve and work on meeting technical, tactical, physical, or mental performance goals. Closing the gap between the

present and the ideal is a continuing
drive for elite athletes of all sports,
especially triathletes.

In assessing and planning for
effective performance, determined
athletes establish training and
performance objectives by (i)
accurately assessing short-term
needs relative to the broader goal
of performing more effectively
and efficiently in competition, (ii)
accessing previous experiences
and sport knowledge to determine
their specific needs, (iii) using
knowledge of the present situation
as well as previous experiences
to make informed decisions and
formulate effective strategy, and
(iv) implementing and refining
these strategies during regular

training. Athletic performance before, during, and after training/
competition is as much an active mental activity as it is a physical one.
It's important to remember that when watching elite triathletes at an
event or on T.V., we're observing the end result of countless hours of
physical and mental experience—that is, the maximized athlete.

Reflection

The process of reflection is an essential ingredient in the maximized
athlete package. Granted, it may be a small ingredient, but it can have
enormous implications for performance development. Incorporating
reflective practice toward triathlon training and competition will allow
you to practice framing problems related to performance. Thoroughly
comprehending and understanding a problem in training can facilitate
the formation of strategies and solutions to modify thought processes
during key points of competition. Further, incorporating reflective skills
on a regular basis will leave you more able to evaluate the results of
training and competition. Reflection can bring positive change in both
the content (i.e., the "how" to train) and the scheduling (i.e., the "when"
to train) of practice. Applying your knowledge and experience together

with a reflective thinking strategy can lead to faster split times, higher placed finishes, and greater satisfaction with your performance.

Two types of reflection are appropriate for triathletes. *Reflection-in-action* refers to the process of interpreting, analyzing, and providing solutions to complex and situational problems during the period of time in which you remain in the same situation (e.g., during the bike leg). *Reflection-on-action* takes place after the event, when you are mentally reconstructing specific situations to analyze your actions and their consequences (e.g., at home following an event).

Reflection-in-action can be difficult to implement, since at some stage you may be attending to many different aspects of performance (e.g., during transitions you attend to the immediate job of changing equipment, refocusing on the new discipline, studying competitors). However, during prolonged stretches of the swim, run, and bike legs, times for reflection can occur. Performance modifications can be made relative to things such as strategy and split time targets. More typically, both athletes and coaches use reflection-on-action following training and competition. This is often in the form of a chat or an unstructured discussion. However, if unstructured, little of this type of reflection is acted upon or considered for future training and triathlon performance. It is recommended that athletes structure reflection-on-action, applying the information gleaned from different forms of reflection. The following are suggestions for structuring reflection-on-action:

1. Designate a time to discuss your performance with fellow athletes (or, ideally, a coach). However, try to avoid reflection immediately after games or training. One or two days following performance is usually most beneficial for accurate reflections. This gives time for a more objective analysis.

2. Plan an agenda for reflection. For example, reflect upon the competition as it progressed or, conversely, start with the finish of the race and reflect back toward the beginning of the race. Doing this will clarify the content of your reflection.

3. Extract key points from the discussion and designate plans of action for training and competition that address these key points.

4. Plan and prepare the most effective ways of training for your performance needs.

Often, communication with coaches and competitors can be effective in stimulating reflection and solution. The procedure of taking 'jot-notes' or audio recordings during communication can help not only in recalling important events or situations for reflection, but also in initiating answers and solutions.

Another effective tool to facilitate structured reflection is a *performance reflection form* (PRF) tailored to your specific needs. Making reflection personally meaningful is important for obtaining the most useful information needed to improve your specific performance. Figures 7.1 and 7.2 provide examples of PRFs designed for triathlon training and competition. The PRF allows reflective thinking to be recorded and utilized in a more informational manner. This information can then be used to plan, evaluate, and set goals in order to optimally prepare for future competitive performances. Generating a file of reflection forms can help create more effective training and performance strategies for forthcoming preparation and competition, as well as for evaluating a season of training and racing.

If you wish to construct your own reflective practice form, here are some questions you may wish to consider for stimulating reflection.

- How did my approach work with the situation?

    - What did I do when strategies did or did not work?

        - How could I improve this situation?

            - Did I implement the right approach at the right time?

            - Did I achieve the goal?

            - What did I learn from the event/section of the race?

        - Did I encounter unexpected obstacles in completing this task?

        - What new goals do I have now?

        - What is the best way to approach them?

        - What is my strategy for next time?

Figure 7.1: The Performance Reflection Form—Training

Date: _____ Aims of the workout session: 1) _____

2) _____

3) _____

Exercises/Drills used:	**Rating (%):**
1) _____	_____
2) _____	_____
3) _____	_____
4) _____	_____
5) _____	_____

Workout positives:

1) _____

2) _____

3) _____

Things to work on:

1) _____

2) _____

3) _____

Lessons learned from the workout:

1) _____

2) _____

3) _____

Comments for self:

_____

_____

_____

_____

_____

_____

Figure 7.2: The Performance Reflection Form—Competition

Date:_____ Pre-race goals: 1)_____

2)_____

3)_____

Rating (%):

Pre-Race   _____

Swim Portion   _____

Swim/Bike Transition   _____

Bike Portion   _____

Bike/Run Transition   _____

Run Portion   _____

Post Race   _____

Race positives:

1) _____

2) _____

3) _____

Things to work on:

1) _____

2) _____

3) _____

Lessons learned from the race:

1) _____

2) _____

3) _____

Comments for self:

_____

_____

_____

If benefits are to accrue, enhancing periods of structured reflection through extensive practice and feedback is critical. Expertise in triathlon as in other domains can only be expected to develop from hours and years actually spent performing the requisite mental and physical skills within the context of the triathlon event.

Reflection, while effectively described as *backward thinking,* (in a good sense!) provides a valuable learning opportunity to formulate strategies for *forward thinking* and improvement. Training and competition underpinned by systematic reflection are essential components of a structured preparation plan to improve performance.

CHAPTER HIGHLIGHTS

• Reflection can be useful in maximizing performance.

• It allows athletes to develop awareness of critical areas where improvement is needed.

• Reflection-in-action is useful for monitoring performance and adjusting goals during competition.

• Reflection-on-action is essential after competition to determine whether goals are met and how to design future training.

[1] The authors would like to acknowledge the significant contribution to this chapter by Stephen Cobley, senior lecturer at Leeds Metropolitan University.

8

STICKING WITH IT: CONCLUDING REMARKS

Until one is committed, there is hesitancy, the chance to draw back, always ineffectiveness. Concerning all acts of initiative and creation, there is one elementary truth the ignorance of which kills countless ideas and splendid plans: that the moment one definitely commits oneself, then providence moves too. All sorts of things occur to help one that would never otherwise have occurred. A whole stream of events issues from the decision, raising in one's favor all manner of unforeseen incidents, meetings, and material assistance which no man could have dreamed would have come his way. Whatever you can do or dream you can, begin it. Boldness has genius, power, and magic in it. Begin it now.

W. H. Murray

The final chapter of this book provides information that can be used to help you stick with your mental fitness plan. One of the key points we made at the beginning of the book was that mental skills, like physical skills, require devoted practice in order to become most effective. This point can't be emphasized enough. Although many of the exercises and approaches discussed in this book may seem straightforward and simple, they require a significant commitment from you in order to work. This is particularly true for skills like imagery, which can be quite difficult to get a handle on at first. There are a number of tips you can use to help yourself stay on task with your mental training.

Keep a Mental Training Log

Keeping a training log for physical workouts is an excellent idea. It helps you monitor progress and stay motivated to continue your training. The same is true for your mental workouts. Keep track of the amount of time you practice your mental skills. You can add this information directly to your normal day-to-day training log so that you get into the habit of adding the details of your mental training at the same time you add your physical training. Journaling at night before falling asleep is one option. Carrying your journal with you during the day to record random thoughts can also be a useful strategy. Some athletes also find accessing their creative sides, such as writing stories or drawing, to be effective.

Structure Your Mental Training into Your Training Schedule

Often athletes wait and try to do their mental training whenever they have time. Would you do the same for your physical training? Likely not. Identify specific times in your training schedule to perform your psychological training. Remember that mental skills, like physical skills, need to be learned. This means regular, daily practice! This means prior to, during, and after training sessions and competitions. Actually slotting in times for your mental training and seeing this on your weekly training schedule increases the likelihood that you will do it.

Use Goal Setting

In our chapter on goal setting we discussed how you could use short- and long-term goals to improve your physical training and performance. The same applies for your mental training. Set short- and long-term goals for this aspect of your training program. What mental goals would you like to accomplish in the next month? In the next 12 months? Use the SMARTER procedure for setting these goals as you would for physical performance goals. Be sure to add a performance review component to your goal-setting plan to examine whether you have achieved your goals or whether they need to be modified.

Get Your Training Partners Involved

Training as part of a group can add an extra element of interest to your training. Group rides or training runs are often more fun and motivating than training alone. With mental training, the same general idea holds although there are some key distinctions. For the most part, your mental training needs to be done alone since it should be a program set up for your specific needs. However, having your training partners involved in their own mental training program will provide you with someone to share ideas with, help solve any problems, and deal with any setbacks. Training partners also help you to stay on task on those days when training is difficult. Just setting up a simple biweekly or monthly meeting to discuss how your mental training is going can help you stay focused and attentive.

Getting Started

It's important to consider when to begin implementing the techniques outlined in this book. While several of the exercises contained in this volume are restricted to problems related to competition, they need to be practiced and honed during the months prior to the start of the competitive season. Just as you would not begin your physical training a few weeks before a big race, you should not expect optimal benefits from your mental training unless you have devoted the required time to its development. Preferably, your mental training should begin during the off-season, when you can concentrate fully on learning new skills without the distraction of upcoming competitions. It can take months

It takes a long time to bring excellence to maturity.
Publilius Syrus

to effectively understand and integrate your new psychological skills into training and competition. Expect that your motivation may vary, but commit to putting one foot in front of the next relative to learning and integrating the new techniques. Using the periodization model we discussed in Chapter 6, mental training should be started in the recovery phase, when your training is less intense and you can devote more effort to learning new skills. By the time the recovery stage is over, you will have many of the kinks worked out of your system, allowing you to focus on using your new skills in the upcoming competitive season. We are confident that with time and effort, you will be able to make these skills work for you. We wish you all the best on this venture.

CHAPTER HIGHLIGHTS

• Acquiring mental skills requires a long-term commitment.

• Use training logs, schedules, goal setting, and training partners to help you stick with your mental skills program.

• Ideally, a mental training program should be begun in the off-season, although it can be beneficial to performance at any time of year.

Further Reading

This section provides a brief list of suggestions for those interested in reading more about the topics presented in this book. This is by no means an exhaustive list, but it will provide a good starting point. Please note the professional journal articles may be a bit too heady for some readers. These articles are included as they reference some of the specific ideas contained in the text.

Triathlon Training - General

Allen, M., & Babbitt, B. (1988). *Mark Allen's total triathlete.* NTC Contemporary Publishing.

Aschwer, H. (2003). *The complete guide to triathlon training.* Lewis International.

Bernhardt, G. (2000). *Training plans for multi-sport athletes.* Boulder, CO: Velopress.

Bompa, T. O. (1999). *Periodization training for sports.* Champaign, IL: Human Kinetics.

Edwards, S. (1992). *Triathlons for women.* Santa Monica, CA: Triathlete Magazine.

Fitzgerald, M. (2003). *Complete triathlon book: The training, diet, health, equipment, and safety tips you need to do your best.* Time Warner Publishing.

Fleck, S. J., & Kraemer, W. J. (1987). *Designing Resistance Training Programs.* Champaign, IL: Human Kinetics.

Friel, J., & Bryne, G. (2003). *Going long: Training for Ironman-distance triathlons.* Boulder, CO: Velopress.

Hellemans, J. (1993). *Triathlon: A complete guide for training and racing.* Reed Publishers: Auckland, New Zealand.

Jonas, S (2002). *The essential triathlete.* Lyons, Press.

Scott, D. (1986). *Dave Scott's triathlon training.* Distican Publishing Inc.

Tinley, S. (1995). *Finding the wheel's hub: Tales and thoughts on the endurance athletic lifestyle.* Trimarket Publishing.

Tinley, S., & Plant, M. (1986). *Scott Tinley's winning triathlon.* NTC Contemporary Publishing.

Sport Psychology - General

Anshel, M. H. (2003). (4th Ed,). *Sport psychology: From theory to practice.* San Francisco; Benjamin Cummings.

Bull, S. J., Albinson, J., & Shambrook, C.J. (1996). *The mental game plan: Getting psyched for sport.* East Sussex, UK: Sports Dynamics.

Elliot, R. (1984). *The competitive edge: Mental training preparation for distance running.* Englewood Cliffs, NJ.: Prentice-Hall.

Hardy, L., Jones, G., & Gould, D. (1996). *Understanding psychological preparation for sport: Theory and practice of elite performers.* Chichester: Wiley.

Miller, S., & Maass Hill, P. (1999). *Sport psychology for cyclists.* Boulder, CO: Velopress.

O'Conner, P. J. (1992). Psychological aspects of endurance performance. In R.J. Shephard and P.O. Astrand (Eds.). *Endurance in Sport.* Oxford: Blackwell Scientific.

Orlick, T. (1986). *Psyching for sport: Mental training for athletes.* Champaign, IL: Human Kinetics.

Orlick, T. (1998). *Embracing your potential.* Champaign, IL: Human Kinetics.

Orlick, T. (2000). *In pursuit of excellence: How to win in sport and life through mental training.* Champaign, IL: Human Kinetics.

Theodorakis, Y., Collins, D.; & Sharp, M. (2000). Expectancy effects and strength training: Do steroids make a difference? *The Sport Psychologist, 14*(3), 272-278.

Vanden Auweele, Y., DeCuyper, B., Van Mele, V., & Rzewnicki, R. (1993). Elite performance and personality: From description and prediction to diagnosis and intervention. In R. N. Singer, M. Murphey, & L. K. Tennant (Eds.), *Handbook of research in sport psychology* (pp. 257-289). New York: Macmillan.

Wann, D. L. (1997). *Sport psychology.* Upper Saddle River, NJ: Prentice Hall.

Weinberg, R. S., & Gould, D. (2003). *Foundations of Sport and Exercise Psychology 3rd Edition.* Champaign, IL: Human Kinetics.

Williams, J. M. (2001). *Applied sport psychology: Personal growth to peak performance 4th Edition.* Mountain View, CA: Mayfield.

Goal Setting and Motivation

Ajzen, I., & Fishbein, M. (1980). *Understanding Attitudes and Predicting Social Behavior.* Englewood Cliffs, NJ: Prentice-Hall.

Ames, C. (1992). Achievement goals, motivational climate, and motivational processes. In G.C. Roberts (Ed.), *Motivation in sport and exercise* (pp. 161-176). Champaign, IL: Human Kinetics.

Burton, D. (1992). The Jekyll/Hyde nature of goals: Reconceptualizing goal setting in sport. In T. S. Horn (Ed.), *Advances in sport psychology* (pp. 267-297). Champaign, IL: Human Kinetics.

Deci, E. L., & Olson, B. C. (1989). Motivation and competition: Their role in sports. In J. H. Goldstein (Ed.), *Sports, games and play: Social and psychological viewpoints.* (2nd ed., pp. 83-110).

Duda, J. L. (1989). The relationship between task and ego orientation and the perceived purpose of sport among male and female high school athletes. *Journal of Sport and Exercise Psychology, 11,* 318-335.

Duda, J. L. (1992). *Motivation in sport settings: A goal perspective approach.* (pp. 57-91). In G. Roberts (Ed.). Motivation in sport and exercise. Champaign, IL: Human Kinetics.

Duffy, E. (1962). *Activation and behavior.* New York: Wiley.

Dweck, C. S. (1986). Motivational processes affecting learning. *American Psychologist, 41,* 1040-1048.

Locke, E. A. (1968). Toward a theory of task motivation incentives. *Organizational Behavior and Human Performance, 3,* 157-189.

Locke, E. A., & Latham, G. P. (1985). The application of goal setting to sports. *Journal of Sport and Exercise Psychology, 7,* 205-222.

Locke, E. A., & Latham, G. P. (1990). *A theory of goal setting and task performance.* Englewood Cliffs, CA: Prentice Hall.

Locke, E. A., & Shaw, K. N., Saari, L. M., & Latham, G. P. (1981). Goal setting and task performance. *Psychological Bulletin, 90,* 125-152.

Naber, J. (1999). *Awaken the Olympian within.* Irvine, CA: Griffin Publishing Group.

Weinberg, R. S., & Weigand, D. (1993). Goal setting in sport and exercise: A reaction to Locke. *Journal of Sport and Exercise Psychology, 15,* 88-96.

Weiner, B. (1986). *An attributional theory of motivation and emotion.* New York: Springer-Verlag.

Imagery and Visualization

Anshel, M. H. (2003). (4th Ed.). *Sport psychology: From theory to practice.* San Francisco: Benjamin Cummings.

Hardy, L., Jones, G., & Gould, D. (1996). *Understanding psychological preparation for sport: Theory and practice of elite performers.* New York: John Wiley & Sons.

Jacobsen, E. (1930). Electrical measurement of neuromuscular states during mental activities. *American Journal of Physiology, 94,* 22-34.

Moran, A.(1996). *The psychology of concentration in sport performers: A cognitive analysis.* East Sussex, UK: Psychology Press.

Murphy, S. M. (1994). Imagery interventions in sport. *Medicine and Science in Sports and Exercise, 26,* 486-494.

Orlick, T., & Partington, J. (1987). The sport psychology consultant: Analysis of critical components as viewed by Canadian Olympic Athletes. *The Sport Psychologist, 1,* 4-17.

Suinn, R. M. (1972a). Behavior rehearsal training for ski races. *Behavior Therapy, 3,* 519-520.

Suinn, R. M. (1972b). Removing obstacles to learning and performance by visuo-motor behaviour rehearsal. *Behavior Therapy, 3,* 308-310.

Weinberg, R. S. (1981). The relationship between mental preparation strategies and motor performance: A review and critique. *Quest, 33,* 195-213.

White, A., & Hardy, L. (1995). Use of different imagery perspectives on the learning and performance of different motor skills. *British Journal of Psychology, 86,* 169-180.

Williams, J. M. (2nd Ed.). (1993). *Applied sport psychology; Personal growth to peak performance.* Mountainview, CA: Mayfield.

Dealing with Anxiety, Arousal, and Stress

Annesi, J. J. (1998). Applications of individual zones of optimal functioning for the multimodal treatment of precompetitive anxiety. *The Sport Psychologist, 12* (3), 300-316.

Hammermeister, J., & Burton, D. (1995). Anxiety and the ironman: Investigating the antecedents and consequences of endurance athletes' state anxiety. *The Sport Psychologist, 9* (1), 29-40.

Hanin, Y. L. (1997). Emotions and athletic performance: Individual zones of optimal functioning. *European Yearbook of Sport Psychology, 1,* 29-72.

Hanin, Y. L. (2000). *Emotions in sport.* Champaign, IL: Human Kinetics.

Hardy, L. (1990). A catastrophe model of anxiety and performance. In J.G. Jones and L. Hardy (Eds.), *Stress and performance in sport.* Chichester: Wiley.

Lane, A. M, Terry, P. C., & Karageorghis, C. I. (1 995). Path analysis examining relationships among antecedents of anxiety and multidimensional state anxiety and triathlon performance. *Perceptual and Motor Skills, 81* (3, Pt.2), 1255-1266.

Lazarus, R. S. (1966). *Psychological stress and coping process.* New York: McGraw Hill.

Martens, R., Vealey, R. S., & Burton, D. (1990). *Competitive anxiety in sport.* Champaign, IL: Human Kinetics.

Morris, L., Davis, D., & Hutchings, C. (1981). Cognitive and emotional components of anxiety: Literature review and revised worry-emotionality scale. *Journal of Educational Psychology, 73,* 541-555.

Oxendine, J. B. (1984). *Psychology of motor learning.* Englewood Cliffs, NJ: Prentice-Hall.

Pribram, K. H., & McGuinness, D. (1975). Arousal, activation and effort in the control of attention. *Psychological Review, 82,* 116-149.

Speilberger, C. D. (1966). Theory and research on anxiety. In C.D. Spielberg (Ed.), *Anxiety and Behavior* (pp. 3-22). New York: Academic Press.

Williams, J. M., Tonymon, P., & Andersen, M. B. (1991). The effects of stressors and coping resources on anxiety and peripheral narrowing. *Journal of Applied Sport Psychology, 3,* 126-141.

Focus and Concentration

Moran, A. (1996). *The psychology of concentration in sport performers: A cognitive analysis.* Mahwah, NJ; Lawrence Erlbaum.

Morgan, W. P., O'Connor, P. J., Ellickson, H. A., & Bradley, P. W. (1988). Personality structure, mood states, and performance in elite distance runners. *International Journal of Sport Psychology, 19,* 247-269.

Morgan, W. P., O'Connor, P. J., Sparling, P. B., & Pate, R. R. (1987). Psychologic characterization of the elite female distance runner. *International Journal of Sports Medicine, 8,* 124-131.

Morgan, W. P., & Pollock, M. L. (1977). Psychologic characterization of the elite distance runner. *Annals of the New York Academy of Science, 301,* 382-403.

Dealing with Pain and Injury - Overtraining Syndrome

Froehlich, J. (1993). Overtraining Syndrome. In J. Heil (Ed.) *Psychology of sport injury.* Champaign, IL: Human Kinetics.

Fry, R. W., Morton, A. R., & Keast, D. (1991). Overtraining in athletes: An update. *Sports Medicine, 12,* 32-65.

Fry, R. W., Morton, A. R., & Keast, D. (1992). Periodisation of training stress: A review. *Canadian Journal of Sport Sciences, 17,* 234-240.

Heil, J. (1993). *Psychology of sport injury.* Champaign, IL: Human Kinetics.

Selye, H. (1976). *The stress of life.* New York: McGraw-Hill.

Turk, D. C., Meichenbaum, D., & Genest, M. (1983). *Pain and behavioral medicine: A cognitive behavioral approach.* New York: Guilford Press.

Reflection and Self-Awareness

Csikszentmihalyi, M. (1993). *The evolving self.* New York: Harper & Row.

Csikszentmihalyi, M. (1997). *Finding flow.* New York: Harper Collins.

Jackson, S. A., & Csikszentmihalyi, M. (1999). *Flow in sports: The keys to optimal experiences and performances.* Champaign, IL: Human Kinetics.

Schon, D. A. (1983). *The reflective practitioner.* New York: Basic Books.

Snyder, C. R., & Lopez, S. J. (2002). *Handbook of positive psychology.* New York: Oxford University Press.

Photo/Illustration Credits

Index

About the Authors

Joe Baker, PhD, is an assistant professor in the School of Kinesiology and Health Sciences at York University, Toronto, Canada. His PhD research examined physiological and psychological components of expertise in Ironman triathletes. Joe has been a triathlete and ultra-runner for more than 15 years, racing triathlon distances from sprint to Ironman. He has published articles on the requirements of successful performance in journals such as the *Journal of Applied Sport Psychology, Research Quarterly for Exercise and Sport, Applied Cognitive Psychology,* and has presented his research at academic conferences around the world. In 2000, Joe was a winner of the Franklin Henry Young Scientist Award by the Canadian Society for Psychomotor Learning and Sport Psychology.

Whitney Sedgwick, PhD, R. Psych., is a psychologist at the University of British Columbia's Counselling Services. Prior to this, she completed a postdoctoral fellowship in the School of Human Kinetics at UBC where she conducted research (primarily on body image) and taught courses in sport psychology. Her research interests include the development of expertise, in both athletes and the practitioners who work with them. Whitney has a master's degree in sport psychology and a doctorate in clinical psychology. She has taught sport science and psychology courses at universities throughout North America. Whitney has also worked as a sport psychology consultant for nine years, including a year at I.N.S.E.P., the French National Sport Institute, in Paris, France. Whitney was a candidate for the Canadian National Rowing team as a coxswain. With a competitive running background, she looks forward to more triathlon racing in the future.